"Insightful and spot on! Nanette cares deeply about the nonprofit sector and has written ... resource to guide boards toward success."
Representative Lori A. Ehrlich, Former President of HealthLink, Inc. and The Environmental Integrity Project

"Too often the expectations of board members and the workings of nonprofits have been vague or mysterious. Whether you are a professional or board member, On Board demystifies how nonprofits work and lays out in detail how board members can be responsible, effective and fulfilled."
Dr. Marc N. Kramer, Executive Director, RAVSAK: The Jewish Community Day School Network

"As a member of multiple nonprofit boards and having been a nonprofit manager myself, I would recommend On Board to anyone who is currently on or is considering joining a board or is looking to start a nonprofit themselves. It is informative and easy to read—a really valuable resource."
Andrea Friedman, Founder, AF Advocacy

"Nanette Fridman insightfully shares her experience with nonprofit boards to help individuals be more intentional, engaged and clear about their roles. Every governance committee should give this book to their new and ongoing board members."
Nancy K. Kaufman, Chief Executive Officer, National Council of Jewish Women

"With On Board, board members—new and experienced—will learn how to be effective stewards, ambassadors and leaders of their organizations."
Judy Neufeld, Former Vice President, Emerge America

"A perfect primer for the novice director and rich refresher for the veteran board member!"
Suzanne Fogarty, Head of Lincoln School

"Nanette Fridman has written a very practical handbook for nonprofit boards filled with lots of useful tips, checklists and examples!"
Beth Kanter, Author, Measuring the Networked Nonprofit

"Even the best executive director can only do so much without a well-functioning board. This book is the perfect companion to any executive director who wants to build their board and drive more change into the communities they serve."
Laura Gassner Otting, President, Nonprofit Professionals Advisory Group

Publishing guidance and process managed by Wordmountain.com
Cover and book design by LisaThompsonGraphicDesign.com

Library of Congress Control Number: 2014919219
ISBN: 9780692306369

Published by Fridman Strategies
Newton, MA

ON BOARD

WHAT CURRENT AND ASPIRING
BOARD MEMBERS MUST KNOW ABOUT
NONPROFITS & BOARD SERVICE

NANETTE R. FRIDMAN

FRIDMAN
STRATEGIES

To my children, Jacob and Alexis:
I love you more than googolplex.

Always remember, "It is not your responsibility to finish the work
of perfecting the world, but you are not free to desist from it either."

ETHICS OF THE FATHERS 2:16.

CONTENTS

1

FOREWORD

"IF YOU WANT TO GO FAST, GO ALONE. IF YOU WANT TO GO FAR, GO TOGETHER." This African proverb and key leadership insight is one I've seen Nanette Fridman put into practice for nonprofit organizations time and time again over the last twenty years. Through her extensive experience working with charities across the country, Nanette knows that most try hard to do good in the world but fewer possess the funding, expertise, and strategies necessary to operate in a sustainable way and accomplish their mission. The most successful nonprofit leaders understand that impacting lives, improving communities, and solving societal problems require success on all fronts and major help from others. This is why every nonprofit needs the guidance and support of a high-functioning board of directors. And this is why every board would be wise to follow the guidance and support provided by Nanette Fridman in *On Board: What Current and Aspiring Board Members Must Know About Nonprofits and Board Service*.

Nanette is one of the smartest people I have ever met. She is an expert on nonprofit leadership with a special talent for helping executives and boards create the right strategies for their unique scenarios and advising on the implementation process as well. With a background in corporate law and public policy, innate leadership skills, and years serving on nonprofit boards, Nanette was bombarded with requests from nonprofits for more help. Thankfully, she realized she could do even more to guide nonprofits in overcoming hurdles and reaching their goals if she opened her own full-time consulting firm, Fridman Strategies. I joined many other nonprofit executives in jumping at the chance to work with her in a deeper way.

When I founded and led a local grassroots, basketball-based mentoring and leadership program for youths in New York City, bringing in Nanette and her expertise was at the top of my to-do list. Her training and guidance helped me and my team build a board, raise funds, improve our program delivery, raise awareness, and build key partnerships to run and expand a program that continues on today.

More recently, I became Executive Vice President—and then President—of the After-School All-Stars National Network. My responsibilities include facilitating the work of fifteen local chapters that provide free daily afterschool programs for 100,000 low-income students in 400 Title I schools across the country. Upon becoming EVP, Nanette Fridman was one of my first calls.

Working within a federated model with many chapters operating as independent 501(c)3 nonprofit organizations is complex. All chapters were unified and consistent in offering high quality, programs from 3:00–6:00 pm at school sites, but they varied in structure, size, and strengths. Some were connected to larger local institutions such as universities and government agencies. Some were twenty years old and others were startups. I knew there was no one-size-fits-all approach to meeting their needs, and we needed someone who could help us tailor our support strategies to the unique circumstances, assets, and talents of each chapter. Nanette was the perfect partner.

For four years, we crossed the country, listening to our local executive directors and board chairs. We learned what they did well, where their pain points were, how to quickly address challenges, and what to avoid. We researched best practices in our field and learned from leaders in other industries and sectors. We took chapter staff and boards through the process of writing long-term strategic plans, developing and meeting their fundraising goals, and running powerful board and staff planning retreats. We developed turnkey solutions, systems, and tools in the areas of fiscal and legal operations, fundraising, marketing, partnerships, staff training, program evaluation, advocacy, planning, and board development so all chapters would be in better position to focus on what they do best—serving youth.

Today, the After-School All-Stars National Network is stronger, more successful, and more sustainable than ever before. Last year, we set records in terms of fundraising; marketing metrics; and positive academic, health and behavior outcomes for students. Our track record, reputation, and momentum led us to receive a multi-million dollar, multi-phase expansion grant that will allow us to double the number of chapters we have and students we serve over the next eight years. Nanette was an integral part of the team that helped us reach this point.

When French author and philosopher Alexis De Tocqueville visited the United States in the late 1800s, he was blown away by what a uniquely civic-minded and philanthropic country this was. In fact, many of today's largest and best-known nonprofits, such as Boys & Girls Clubs, Rotary, NAACP, Big Brothers, Big Sisters, Red Cross, Good Will, and United Way were established over a thirty-year period between 1890 and 1920. Civic leaders then recognized the new challenges arising in the US due to large-scale immigration, urbanization, and industrialization and realized they needed powerful new nonprofit organizations to offer solutions.

Over the last thirty years, cuts to government funding and programs, new technology and a more socially entrepreneurial citizenry have led to another huge growth spurt in the nonprofit sector. Research shows we now have more than 1.5 million different nonprofits in the US responding to increased demand for services. All compete for limited dollars, media attention, and resources. Unfortunately, the number of *funders* in the United States has not grown at the same pace. I believe the difference between the nonprofits that will fail and the ones that will thrive will come down to this: the leadership, planning, and effectiveness of their boards.

Open any newspaper or watch the nightly news—it is clear that we continue to live in a troubled world. Challenges in areas such as education, environment, health care, economy, public safety, international conflicts, and political gridlock have made the important work that nonprofits do more critical and urgent than ever before.

Nonprofit boards have the power to guide, unite, build, and mobilize leaders from every sector to work together on new solutions to long-time problems. Inspired individuals willing to come together to donate their time, talents, and treasure to help do-good organizations grow and succeed are fundamental to our country's future success. With help from *On Board*, executive directors and boards will have a clear roadmap for becoming more effective and efficient, navigating obstacles, and, of course, taking their organizations further than they ever dreamed possible.

Aaron Philip Dworkin
President, After-School All-Stars National Network
Washington, DC
September 2014

PREFACE

I love my job. As a trainer and consultant to nonprofit boards large and small, I help nonprofits perform at their best, taking strategic action in planning, fundraising, and governing. I've seen first-hand—in ways you might expect and ways you might never imagine—how a well-functioning board can meet the objectives of their mission and do good in the world.

And it never gets boring!

During my twenty plus years of involvement with the nonprofit sector, I have found meaning and purpose. While serving as a volunteer, board member, staff member, consultant, and trainer, I have forged common ground with fellow colleagues and clients, made dear friends, and found important mentors. I got lucky—I found my calling.

In writing this book, I engaged many of these people in revealing discussions about the critical role of nonprofit boards and about the frustrations and the missed opportunities that occur when board members take a seat at the table and don't do much else—or worse, distract the organization from its important work. I've learned how to change that and want to share with volunteers and staff in the nonprofit sector as much as I can—through this book, board training, and consultation.

Throughout my years of training boards—at *dozens* of nonprofits— board members have often shared that they are told little of their roles and responsibilities, either before or after they join the board. Would you ever hire someone for a job without explaining his or her duties?

The bottom line and my mantra throughout this book:

A nonprofit is only as effective as its board.

My motivation for writing this guide is to make crystal clear to present and potential board members the most important aspects of their roles, both in word and in practice. Their actions matter! Nonprofits need people to assume their roles with clarity and intentionality and to commit to contributing their talents and passion. As a society, we have too many important issues to tackle—and so many people who depend on the services and who are enriched by the programs that nonprofits provide—to waste a moment or an opportunity.

I invite you to connect with me via e-mail or social media. I will be happy to respond to your questions and hear your thoughts. My only objective—which I'm sure is yours as well—is to make your nonprofit board service as enjoyable and rewarding as it can be.

Nanette Fridman
Founder and Principal, Fridman Strategies
E-mail: fridmanstrategies@gmail.com
Twitter: @NanetteFridman
Facebook: https://www.facebook.com/FridmanStrategies
LinkedIn: www.linkedin.com/in/nanettefridman/
Website: www.fridmanstrategies.com

INTRODUCTION

A few words on the title: *On Board.*

Board is used in the English language in so many ways (in addition to talking about a piece of wood!). One is as I use it in this book: *serving on a board of directors* of a nonprofit. (A for-profit corporation has a board of directors as well, but it is a very different type of leadership from that at a nonprofit—and we'll get into the differences between the two). There is also *onboarding*—getting a new hire ready to contribute to the organization's work. And finally, there is *boarding* as it relates to getting on a plane, train, bus, or ship.

All these people have one thing in common when they board, join a board, or are onboarded:

They are moving in the same direction.

That's what this book is about—to ensure that nonprofit board members are all on board—moving in the same direction toward a common goal that serves the greater good.

I've trained thousands of board members and served on many boards myself. And in my experience, the most effective boards are composed of informed board members who are given the tools, information, and leadership to make great things happen!

Serving on a nonprofit board should be an enriching experience and a memorable journey. It's a chance for you to expand both your personal and professional horizons and to make a contribution to your community. It's an opportunity to work with others on a worthy cause and to see the results of your efforts.

No journey should be undertaken without a map or a guidebook. This is your guide to the land of board service.

In these pages you'll find everything you need to begin and enjoy your adventure. It has been written for the first-time board member as well as the seasoned veteran. It's for the reader who serves on the board of a small community nonprofit and the reader who serves on the board of a national service organization, major university, or big-city hospital.

In this book I reveal the inner workings of nonprofit boards—the committee structure, how meetings are conducted, and how members are chosen. I explain what's expected of you as a board member, including donations and committee service. You'll learn how the board works with the executive director, staff, and volunteers. We'll discuss ethical questions and how to approach conflicts and we will review examples of board problems and examine how they might have been avoided.

I'll also share what often goes on behind the scenes at nonprofits, including topics such as fundraising, succession, and working with other board members—even the high-maintenance ones!

You'll learn what information board members should be given but frequently are not, as well as what they want to know but often don't ask. You'll also discover the things that staff members want to say but sometimes just can't.

There is no right way or wrong way to use this book. Depending on the particular circumstance, it may be used it in various ways:

- Research for individuals considering nonprofit board service

- Gifting copies to nominated board members from leadership development committees

- Recommended reading for board members when installed or at annual meetings

- Advanced or supplemental reading for board orientations, trainings, or retreats

- A guide for boards experiencing crisis or change in leadership, structure, circumstances, or direction

- As a fundraising primer

- Assigned by the board chair to underperforming boards as a group read

- Guidance for improving clarity around staff and board roles and improving relationships between both

- Reading for staff responsible for managing the board

- Board–chair leadership circles

- Individuals organizing new nonprofits

...and, of course, anyone who wishes to understand nonprofit governance.

In the pages ahead, I'm going to walk you through everything you need to know both before and once you make your decision to serve. If I make a point that you already understand, simply skip ahead. The goal is for you to be well informed and confident.

Bonuses: There are a several places in the book where you will find the password to our private download area where, as a purchaser of this book, you have access to some of the materials I share with nonprofits during trainings and consultations. But you'll have to keep reading to find the password!

I hope that *On Board* will become your faithful reference—one that you will recommend to your friends and colleagues who are invited to join a nonprofit board or who already serve.

I wish you success in your nonprofit journey. ○

Life's most persistent and urgent question is,
"What are you doing for others?"

~ MARTIN LUTHER KING, JR.

1

THE NONPROFIT SECTOR: A 10,000-FOOT VIEW

The best way to predict the future is to create it.

~ PETER DRUCKER

The phone rings. You answer it. Your friend or business colleague is calling.

"Last night I was at the monthly meeting of the board of directors of the Sunrise Charitable Foundation." There is a touch of excitement in her voice. "And when the leadership development committee made their report, your name came up."

"I'm very flattered," you reply.

"In fact," continues your friend, "I've been asked to give you a call and offer you a seat on the board."

"I'm very grateful for the opportunity. Can I think about it for a few days? I want to be sure I'm making the right decision."

"Of course," says your friend. "We'd like to have the new board in place by next month. Is that enough time?"

"Sounds good," you answer. "I'll get back to you within a week."

The Sunrise Charitable Foundation could be any nonprofit organization—a prestigious art museum, a hospital, a local community group, or your neighborhood house of worship. You probably know of several nonprofits in your city or town that perform good works and that have boards of directors on which you might be asked to serve.

Perhaps serving on the board is something that you've been working towards for a long time. On the other hand, the call from your friend may be unexpected. "Who, me?" you think as you hang up the phone.

Yes, they want you.

Regardless of the size or scope of the organization, you know that accepting a seat on the board means that you are committing to doing the very best job you can to help the organization serve its constituency.

You really want to add value, to contribute, to make a difference.

To do so—to be successful—you must have a solid understanding of how nonprofits operate and the role of the board both in theory and in practice.

Let's start with the birds-eye view.

THE NONPROFIT ORGANIZATION

Most organizations—whether they are nonprofits, private companies, or large public companies—have some sort of *board of directors*. Banks, airlines, churches, synagogues, hospitals, computer companies, soft-drink manufacturers, the local homeless shelter—all of them have a body of elected or appointed members who jointly oversee long-term activities.

Other names for this group of people include board of regents, board of governors, board of managers, board of trustees, and board of visitors. They're close to being the same thing, with some subtle differences. For example, the word *trustee* may have a separate meaning under state law; it may be defined as "a person, association, corporation, or other entity holding property for, or solicited for, any charitable purpose, such as a trustee of a charitable trust." Many states have charitable trust acts or similar laws, separate and distinct from nonprofit corporation acts. The fiduciary standards of a trustee under most charitable trust laws are often interpreted as holding the trustee to a higher standard of conduct than that which is applicable to the director of a nonprofit organization.

Given these and other distinctions, when referring to individuals serving on the governing board of a nonprofit corporation, the general trend is to encourage use of the title of *director* as opposed to trustee.

This book focuses on the boards of *nonprofit* organizations. In the United States, *nonprofit* is the term most commonly used to mean that the organization has applied for—and received—an exemption from paying federal income taxes from the Internal Revenue Service (IRS).

TAX STATUS

To get an exemption from paying federal income tax, a nonprofit organization must meet certain IRS standards. In its guidelines, the IRS states the following:

"To be tax-exempt under section 501(c)(3) of the Internal Revenue Code, an organization must be organized and operated exclusively for exempt purposes set forth in section 501(c)(3), and none of its earnings may inure to any private shareholder or individual. In addition, it may not be an action organization, i.e., it may not attempt to influence legislation as a substantial part of its activities and it may not participate in any campaign activity for or against political candidates."

What are "exempt purposes?" you ask. Here's what the IRS says about that:

"The exempt purposes set forth in section 501(c)(3) are charitable, religious, educational, scientific, literary, testing for public safety, fostering national or international amateur sports competition, and preventing cruelty to children or animals. The term "charitable" is used in its generally accepted legal sense and includes relief of the poor, the distressed, or the underprivileged; advancement of religion; advancement of education or science; erecting or maintaining public buildings, monuments, or works; lessening the burdens of government; lessening neighborhood tensions; eliminating prejudice and discrimination;

defending human and civil rights secured by law; and combating community deterioration and juvenile delinquency."

Basically, the rationale for exemption of an organization from paying federal tax is simply this: the organization is providing a community service that the government, with its tax dollars, would otherwise have to provide. These charitable services can include anything from culture to public health to spiritual guidance. Governments increasingly rely on nonprofits to deliver these services. Likewise, many nonprofits depend on revenues from government contracts and grants to finance their activities and expand their reach. The *Urban Institute's 2010 National Survey of Nonprofit-Government Contracting and Grants* revealed that nearly 33,000 human-service nonprofits had government contracts and grants in 2009, which provided the largest single source of revenue for 62 percent of them. The nearly 200,000 federal, state, and local contracts totaled about $100 billion. That's a big commitment on behalf of the federal government!

There is growing popular opinion that the private sector—both commercial and nonprofit—can be more efficient and effective than government and that while government should consider overall solutions to social-service delivery, or at least facilitate the delivery of these services, the private sector should do the heavy lifting.

But don't think that an IRS tax-exempt designation means that an organization need not file a tax return! Organizations with $50,000 or more in gross receipts are required to file a Form 990 or Form 990-EZ. Organizations with less than $50,000 are required to file an information return known as the Form 990-N (e-Postcard). All private foundations, regardless of size, are required to file a Form 990-PF.

It's time for a little terminology clarification. According to the IRS guidelines, nonprofit status is a *state-law concept*. Nonprofit status may make an organization eligible for certain benefits, such as state sales, property, and income tax exemptions. Although most federal tax-exempt organizations are nonprofit organizations, organizing as a nonprofit organization at the *state* level does not automatically grant the organization exemption from *federal* income tax. Organizations seeking full nonprofit status must apply at both the federal and state levels.

To qualify as exempt from federal income tax, an organization must meet requirements set forth in the Internal Revenue Code. Notwithstanding these subtle differences, in this book, I'll use the convenient umbrella term *nonprofit* to describe any tax-exempt charitable organization.

In addition to not paying federal taxes, there are other differences between a nonprofit organization and a for-profit corporation. In terms of corporate accounting, if an organization has been granted 501(c)(3) tax-exempt status, it means that no profits may be distributed to individuals; all profits must be retained by the organization.

Profits are not related to revenues, cash flow, or assets. Myth buster: working at a nonprofit does not mean that staff members cannot receive generous salaries. As we'll see later in the book, some nonprofit executive salaries are impressive indeed.

As of this writing, the wealthiest nonprofit organization in the United States is Harvard University, with an endowment valued at $32 billion. Nonprofits can be huge, like Harvard or the American Red Cross, which has an annual budget in the range of $3.5 billion. Or they might be tiny, like your community food bank, whose budget consists of whatever happens to be in the cash box stashed in the drawer of the director's desk. In the eyes of the IRS, both of these organizations are performing work that benefits the general public and for which the organization deserves to be tax exempt.

On the other hand, for-profit corporations like Target and Pizza Hut may bring pleasure to people and may even sell a necessary commodity, such as food, but they are organized for the sole purpose of returning a cash profit to their owner, investors, or stockholders. They are not "lessening the burdens of government." Like nonprofits, they are in it to win it, but only for themselves.

In terms of income, a nonprofit can charge for its services and even sell products that directly relate to its charitable mission. But there's one big difference between for-profit and nonprofit organizations: nonprofits can solicit gifts. Individuals can give money to a nonprofit as a donation for which nothing is given in return, and this donation can be claimed on the donor's federal income tax as a taxable income deduction. As the IRS says, "Organizations described in section 501(c)(3), other than testing for public safety organizations, are eligible to receive tax-deductible contributions in accordance with Code section 170." This means that nonprofit organizations are able to attract donated income because donations often don't cost the donor anything; the IRS allows the donor to deduct the amount from their taxable income (assuming itemization and other qualifications). This reduces the amount of tax owed by the donor, creating a win/win situation for all.

THE GROWTH OF THE NONPROFIT SECTOR

Nonprofits have become both big business and a vital part of making societal contributions in the United States. Hospitals, houses of worship, museums, schools and colleges, community health centers, libraries, environmental organizations, cultural centers—there's a good chance that you regularly interact with a nonprofit organization.

Consider the following big-picture survey (Get ready for some stats!).

According to *The Nonprofit Almanac 2012*, prepared by the National Center for Charitable Statistics and published by the Urban Institute Press, an estimated 2.3 million nonprofit organizations operate in the United States; of these, approximately 1.6 million nonprofits were registered with the Internal Revenue Service in 2010. The difference in number between registered organizations and those that are not registered with the IRS includes organizations with less than $5,000 in annual revenue and religious congregations and their auxiliary groups, which are not required by law to register. These 1.6 million nonprofits encompass a wide variety of organizations, including education, arts, health, and advocacy organizations; labor unions; and business and professional associations.

In 2010, the nonprofit sector contributed $804.8 billion to the United States economy, making up 5.5 percent of the nation's gross domestic product. Public charities, the largest component of the nonprofit sector, reported $1.51 trillion in revenue, $1.45 trillion in expenses, and $2.71 trillion in assets.

In 2011, an estimated 26.8 percent of adults in the United States volunteered with a nonprofit organization. Volunteers contributed 15.2 billion hours, worth an estimated $296.2 billion. In that same year, private charitable contributions, including donations to public charities and religious congregations, totaled $298.42 billion.

Most public charities are small; three-quarters of public charities report less than $100,000 in gross receipts, and collectively they represent less than 3 percent of total public charity expenditures. The public-charity economy is dominated by a small number of organizations, primarily higher-education institutions and hospitals; just 4 percent of nonprofits report $10 million or more in expenses, but this 4 percent accounts for more than 85 percent of public-charity expenditures.

NONPROFIT BOARDS VS. CORPORATE BOARDS

A board of directors is responsible for the oversight of an organization's long-term operations, in both the corporate and the nonprofit setting. These are typical duties of a board of directors:

- Setting the strategic direction of the organization

- Governing the organization by establishing policies and objectives

- Selecting, appointing, supporting, and reviewing the performance of the chief executive

- Providing proper financial oversight

- Ensuring adequate financial resources

- Accounting to the stakeholders for the organization's performance

How Nonprofit Boards Differ from Corporate Boards

There are a few major differences between boards of nonprofit organizations and for-profit corporations.

Nonprofit boards are made up of unpaid volunteers.

The board chair and the executive director, who holds the top paid staff position and who may also have the title of chief executive officer (CEO) or president, are typically separate people; few, if any, staff members are also board members. Some organizations require a donation from new and current board members. Many boards emphasize fundraising, and their members' diverse backgrounds lead to broader ownership of the organization and, sometimes, greater stakeholder activism.

In contrast, for-profit board members are paid, some more that what small nonprofits might receive in funding in a year!

Typically, the ranks of corporate boards are filled by CEOs and retired executives. Aside from a handful of board and committee meetings, corporate directorships typically demand little time. A recent study by the National Association of Corporate Directors found directors averaging just 4.3 hours a week on board activities.

In a corporate setting, the board chair and CEO are often the same person. Top company executives often sit on corporate boards. These individuals are called *inside directors,* as opposed to people who have no connection to the company, who are called *outside directors.* Corporate board members have no fundraising responsibility; however, they may represent financial interests that have brought capital funds to the firm.

The scope and focus of a board's fiduciary duty also varies between the corporate world and nonprofit sector. This obligation, which refers to a board's legal duty to act solely in another party's interest, is owed to the company's shareholders in the corporate world and is focused on ensuring that the value of shareholders' investment in the company is preserved and growing. For traditional corporations, the company's social responsibilities are secondary, if at all. This is changing with the rise of Benefit Corporations, or B-Corps.

Benefit Corporations

Benefit corporations originated in Maryland in 2010, based on the idea that some companies are becoming a hybrid of for-profit entities that offer some tangible public benefit. B-corps define success as doing well *and* doing good. While relatively immature in terms of case law, B-corps are increasing in popularity and include many well-known businesses, such as Patagonia, Method Products and Warby Parker. These organizations bridge the gap between for-profit companies, which may sometimes be forced to refrain from certain social initiatives in favor of the bottom line, and nonprofit companies, which are often restricted in their ability to raise capital to grow. Statutes authorizing B-corporations differ by state. Generally speaking, the three common features of all B-corps include the (1) desire to create a material public benefit, (2) the expansion of the company's fiduciary duty to require consideration of non-financial societal and environmental interests, and (3) the publication of an annual benefit report on its overall societal and environmental impact using third-party standards.

Board Member Donations

In the nonprofit realm, the directors' fiduciary duties are twofold. Not unlike the board of a for-profit corporation, the nonprofit board must keep the organization solvent, which means ensuring that the budget is balanced at the end of each year. But at a nonprofit, the mission of the organization is to fulfill its social responsibilities, not turn a profit. The board meets this obligation by ensuring that the organization continues to serve its mission, whatever it may be—spiritual guidance, keeping youth off the streets, or protecting the environment.

Board members of a nonprofit are not motivated by money—they are not getting paid and, in fact, may be required to make a minimum donation to the organization every year.

The National Board Governance Survey for Not-for-Profit Organizations, conducted by the accounting firm Grant Thornton LLP, found that 56 percent of all nonprofits require donations from board members, either personally or by soliciting contributions from their friends and contacts. The size of the mandatory contribution correlated roughly to the size of organization. For nonprofits with annual budgets less than $20 million, 54 percent asked for a minimum of $1,000 or less, while only 14 percent required at least $5,000. On the other end of the scale, 38 percent of nonprofits with budgets more than $500 million required at least a $5,000 contribution, with the rate rising to 60 percent for those in the $100 million to $500 million bracket.

At blue-chip nonprofits, the price tag for board membership can be steep. At the Women and Public Policy Program at Harvard's Kennedy School, each board member is required to "engage philanthropically" with the Women and Public Policy Program, through either his or her company or personally with a minimum annual contribution of $10,000. Sound steep? Try to join the most prestigious nonprofit boards. *The New York Times* reported that to join the power elite at the Metropolitan Museum of Art, you'll need to write a check for as much as $10 million. Ditto for the Museum of Modern Art, while at the New York Public Library it's roughly $5 million. "For those who can, we have an expectation and we try to be very clear about that expectation," said Reynold Levy, the president of Lincoln Center, where the board members are generally asked to contribute $250,000—both upfront and on an annual basis.

At the very highest levels, the donations are breathtaking. In March 2010 *The New York Times,* the reported that philanthropist Ann Ziff had given $30 million to the Metropolitan Opera—the largest single gift from an individual in its history! At the time of her donation, Ziff was the secretary of the Met's board. The Met promptly announced that she would become co-chairwoman of the board in May of that year, before assuming the role of chairwoman the following year.

Generally, it's not always necessary to write a personal check. At some nonprofits, the concept is known as "give, get, or get off." If you can't personally donate, you need to be able to either fundraise it from some other source—your company, usually—or provide some sort of in-kind contribution, such as legal services.

Even in small nonprofits, requiring a personally meaningful, even if token, contribution from each board member can have practical value. Board members are often asked to make an annual donation so that when the organization applies for grant funding, it can report 100 percent board-member support. It's something that charitable foundations like to see before they commit to a sizable grant.

Essentially, the expectation is that if you've been asked to join a nonprofit board, you'll be expected to make a contribution in the form of a donation, your professional services, and/or time devoted to fundraising or work on a board committee. The organization should tell you about all of its board requirements explicitly and up front.

Now let's take a closer look at the role of the nonprofit board and its relationship to the organization which it serves. O

2

....

THE ROLE OF THE NONPROFIT BOARD

If you want to change the world, be that change.

~ MAHATMA GANDHI

So, back to you. In Chapter 1, you were just offered a seat on the board of the Sunrise Charitable Foundation.

While you know a few things about Sunrise, you're not sure what a nonprofit board actually does. You don't know how much of a time commitment you'll need to make nor what the scope of your responsibilities will be. You may fear that once they "reel you in," you'll be expected to join multiple committees, do volunteer work, and even (oh no) ask your friends and colleagues to donate money to the organization.

Relax—you're not alone! For a variety of reasons, many board members don't know what is expected of them, may not fully understand the nonprofit world, and may even feel that the organization is constantly making demands of them. This, in turn, can lead to frustration on the part of the professional staff, which needs to enlist the help of board members.

To understand the role of the board, let's look at the structure and components of nonprofit organizations.

THE MISSION STATEMENT

Every nonprofit charitable organization exists to fulfill a broad goal—a mission—described in general terms in a mission statement.

A well-thought-out mission statement summarizes the organization's purpose and specifies one or more goals that are clear yet flexible enough to allow for operational variations as conditions change. Mission statements can also articulate the means used to achieve the goals and the primary constituents served. The best ones are clear, memorable, and concise.

Here are a few examples:

United Way: "United Way improves lives by mobilizing the caring power of communities around the world to advance the common good."

The Anti-Defamation League: "To stop the defamation of the Jewish people and to secure justice and fair treatment to all."

Juvenile Diabetes Research Foundation: "To find a cure for diabetes and its complications through the support of research."

American Society for the Prevention of Cruelty to Animals (ASPCA): "To provide effective means for the prevention of cruelty to animals throughout the United States."

Public Broadcasting System: "To create content that educates, informs and inspires."

Bill & Melinda Gates Foundation: "Guided by the belief that every life has equal value, the Bill & Melinda Gates Foundation works to help all people lead healthy, productive lives. In developing countries, it focuses on improving people's health and giving them the chance to lift themselves out of hunger and extreme poverty. In the United States, it seeks to ensure that all people—especially those with the fewest resources—have access to the opportunities they need to succeed in school and life."

In the spirit of sharing mission statements, here's ours:

Fridman Strategies: "To help nonprofit organizations and their leaders be more strategic, effective, and efficient."

In addition to the key elements set out here, a mission statement may also address the following issues: Who are the beneficiaries of the organization's work? What makes the organization unique? What is the problem or need that's being addressed? Note, as well, that mission statements may be augmented by additional expressions, such as a values statement and other explanatory materials that describe what activities or programs have been chosen in order to fulfill the organization's purpose.

As a board member, it is important that you understand that the mission statement is the compass that should guide every long-range decision the organization makes. If a new project is proposed, there should be board-level discussions about whether the project is consistent with the organization's mission. If the proposed project does not fit within the organizations mission, it is up to the board to make a difficult choice: whether or not to pursue the project and/or expand the mission. Revising an organization's mission statement generally takes many months and involves soliciting input from the organization's stakeholders—staff, volunteers, and constituents.

Decisions regarding which activities to pursue can also have significant ramifications, even with the IRS. For example, a museum that opens an onsite restaurant for the convenience of visitors and to provide a source of revenue may be required to declare restaurant revenues as taxable income. This is because the IRS doesn't consider the restaurant component of the museum's operations to be part of the museum's mission to enrich the cultural lives of its constituents. On the other hand, a nonprofit soup kitchen or food pantry may have food distribution as its primary charitable mission.

The Vision Statement

The goal of the nonprofit is to affect change in the world.

While the mission statement tends to describe *actions,* the vision statement identifies the *destination.* It defines what the organization plans and hopes to do and become.

Board members usually adopt aspirational vision statements that set the gold standard for the best the organization can become.

Here are a few examples of actual nonprofit vision statements:

ASPCA: "That the United States is a humane community in which all animals are treated with respect and kindness."

Habitat for Humanity: "A world where everyone has a decent place to live."

Make-A-Wish: "Our vision is that people everywhere will share the power of a wish."

The Nature Conservancy: "Our vision is to leave a sustainable world for future generations."

Teach for America: "One day, all children in this nation will have the opportunity to attain an excellent education."

THE VALUES STATEMENT

While the mission statement tends to express action, and the vision statement describes the destination, the values statement conveys the characteristics, traits, and qualities with which an organization wants to be identified. It is the expression of how the organization intends to operate in terms of its ethics and practices. What are the basic values that guide the organization's members in performing their work?

Remember that there are no hard-and-fast rules. Not all organizations have value statements, and some include thoughts about their values in their mission statements.

Below are two examples of actual nonprofit values statements:

ASPCA: "Be good to animals: Act kindly and think progressively to improve the lives of animals. Partner with people: Harness the creativity and passion of people through collaboration and teamwork. Lead responsibly with compassion: Inspire trust through leadership that balances the head and heart."

While the ASPCA statement is brief, the Mayo Clinic offers a detailed list:

Mayo Clinic: "These values, which guide Mayo Clinic's mission to this day, are an expression of the vision and intent of our founders, the original Mayo physicians and the Sisters of Saint Francis.

Respect
Treat everyone in our diverse community, including patients, their families and colleagues, with dignity.

Compassion
Provide the best care, treating patients and family members with sensitivity and empathy.

Integrity
Adhere to the highest standards of professionalism, ethics and personal responsibility, worthy of the trust our patients place in us.

Healing
Inspire hope and nurture the well being of the whole person, respecting physical, emotional and spiritual needs.

Teamwork
Value the contributions of all, blending the skills of individual staff members in unsurpassed collaboration.

Excellence
Deliver the best outcomes and highest-quality service through the dedicated effort of every team member.

Innovation
Infuse and energize the organization, enhancing the lives of those we serve, through the creative ideas and unique talents of each employee.

Stewardship
Sustain and reinvest in our mission and extended communities by wisely managing our human, natural and material resources."

The key takeaway here is that while every nonprofit organization must have a guiding statement, the form it takes is variable, and there is no one-size-fits-all solution. Whatever the statement or statements may be, they should reflect the reality of what the organization can realistically hope to accomplish.

THE NONPROFIT'S SERVICES

A nonprofit fulfills its mission by doing something—providing a good or service or trying to educate the public or decision makers about a particular issue—for the benefit of an intended population, often described in its mission statement. Its target population can be general, like a museum that exists to provide access to fine art to the public at large, or it can be specific, as in the case of a children's advocacy organization that provides legal services and advocacy for at-risk children.

Organizations are sometimes paid for their offerings, as in the case of people buying tickets to attend a concert or museum. In other instances, the purpose of the nonprofit is to offer its services and goods for free: meals offered by a soup kitchen, temporary housing arranged by a homeless shelter, or legal services provided by a legal-aid society. Nonprofits can often sell some services for a profit to offset the costs of providing others with the same or a different service for free; an example of this is a thrift shop.

Some other services, programs, and, efforts include the following:

• Disaster relief for those affected by natural or man-made catastrophes by a charity

• Spiritual guidance and services offered by a house of worship

• Health services provided by a hospital or clinic

• Education provided by a college or training center

- After school programming available for at-risk youth

- Beach cleanups organized by an environmental organization

- Funding for projects granted by a charitable foundation

- Educating the media and decision makers about a policy issue

- Access to recreation, athletic programs, and informal education instruction offered by a community center

- Professional networking and development through involvement in a professional or trade association

It is the board's responsibility to ensure that the organization's activities are successfully furthering its stated mission.

REVENUES

Just as in any business, providing goods and services to the community costs money for a nonprofit. Expenses incurred by a nonprofit may include the facility (hospital, museum, store front), office costs, staff, utilities, materials used, insurance, and much more.

The term *nonprofit* does not mean that you need to provide goods and services for free. Nonprofits get income in many of the same ways that for-profits do. They charge fees for direct services (such as medical care) and for education programs (like the evening programs you take at the art museum). They may charge annual membership fees or one-time entrance fees for programs or exhibits. A nonprofit may have an endowment, which is basically a pool of assets that is maintained on a long-term basis. As of this writing, the largest nonprofit endowment is held by Harvard University; its portfolio of real estate, cash, and securities is valued currently at $32 billion. If it generated just 2 percent per year, this endowment would throw off $64 million in income.

Nonprofits may receive contracts or subsidies from government agencies. They may also solicit and receive donations. Some nonprofits rely heavily on tax-deductible gifts, while others not so much. Donations to nonprofits range in size from a coin tossed into the Salvation Army bucket during the holidays to single gifts that are truly breathtaking. According to a report by the *Chronicle of Philanthropy*, in 2013 Facebook-founder Mark Zuckerberg and his wife, physician Priscilla Chan, gave $992.2 million to the Silicon Valley Community Foundation in Mountain View, California. On the list of the most generous Americans of that year, they were both the number-one donors and the youngest.

According to *"The Nonprofit Sector in Brief: Public Charities, Giving, and Volunteering,"* by the Urban Institute (2012), here's the average breakdown of revenue sources for United States public charities in 2010:

1. Fees for services and goods from private sources: 49.6%, which includes payments to organizations offering services, such as hospitals, health clinics, and child daycare centers

2. Fees for services and goods from government sources: 23.9%, which includes grants and money appropriated by the government for services, such as Medicare and Medicaid

3. Private contributions: 13.3%, which includes grants and donations from individuals, foundations, corporations, and bequests

4. Government grants: 8.3% %, which includes investment income

5. Other: 2.1%

Part of the board's responsibility is to ensure that revenues are adequate to meet the organization's budget requirements each year. If at some point during the year it becomes apparent that revenues are falling short, the board may face the choice of cutting expenses, increasing revenues through gifts, or doing a combination of both.

PAID PROFESSIONAL STAFF

Except for the very smallest community nonprofits, most organizations have at least one paid employee, whether full time or part time. A nonprofit needs paid employees to open the doors every day, collect revenues, pay the bills, maintain the building, and oversee the activities of volunteers. In a typical small nonprofit that has an annual budget of $300,000, there might be an executive director, an office assistant, a maintenance person, and someone who runs the education programs. At the community level, salaries are modest as compared to those in corporate America; depending of the geographical location and size of the organization, the executive director might be paid $50,000. Other staff members might be part time.

One of the largest nonprofits is the American Red Cross, which has roughly 30,000 employees, supplemented by 500,000 volunteers, including Femacorps and Americorps members, who train almost twelve million people in necessary medical skills. According to its IRS Form 990, in 2012 the board of governors of the Red Cross included twenty volunteers who reported an average of four hours commitment per week. The twenty-five-member board also included five members of the organization's professional staff, including President and CEO Gail McGovern, who earned $564,864 for her sixty-hour workweek.

At a large nonprofit, top management salaries may be competitive with those in the private sector. Harvard's president, Drew Gilpin Faust, makes roughly $900,000 a year, which is more than double that of President Barack Obama's salary of $400,000, but a pittance when compared to a very highly paid nonprofit CEO, such as University of Chicago's Robert Zimmer, who in 2011 pulled in over $3.4 million.

Here's another example. According to the *American Institute of Philanthropy*, in 2013 the highest nonprofit salary was $2.2 million; it was paid to Peter T. Scardino, M.D., chairman of attending surgery at Sloan-Kettering Cancer Center. Coming in second was Michael Friedman, M.D., the CEO of City of Hope, a cancer research hospital in

Southern California. While these figures pale in comparison with what people earn at the top of the private sector (in 2013 the CEO with the highest base salary was Tesla Motors CEO Elon Musk, who, thanks to rising stock values, took home $78.2 million), they're still substantial.

VOLUNTEERS

Most nonprofits depend upon the services of volunteers. In addition to the volunteer board members, people donating time to the organization perform many roles: guides, shop attendants, education-program assistants, greeters, fundraisers, accountants, graphic designers, grant writers, legal advisors, and others. Volunteers include student interns, retired folks, professionals, stay-at-home parents—anyone at all who has an interest in the organization's mission.

Volunteers are critical to the health and success of the nonprofit sector. According to *Independent Sector,* in 2010 nonprofits in the United States employed 13.7 million individuals, approximately 10 percent of the country's workforce. In 2011, an estimated 26.8 percent of adults in the United States volunteered with a nonprofit organization contributing 15.2 billion hours and producing an estimated value of $296.2 billion.

A nonprofit will typically use the value of volunteer time to demonstrate to both grant-making foundations and individual donors the level of support the organization receives from their communities. In monetary terms, according to the *Independent Sector,* in 2013 the average value of volunteer time was estimated to be $22.55 per hour.

Organized Pro Bono Volunteers

Pro bono service—professional work undertaken voluntarily and without payment—is one of the largest forms of philanthropy in the country. With the growth in nonprofits, it was inevitable that there would arise organizations dedicated to providing volunteer services on an institutional level—sort of like a temporary employment agency that you don't have to pay or that you pay at a drastically reduced rate.

Founded in 2001 in San Francisco, California, Taproot is a nonprofit organization that makes business talent available to organizations working to improve society. The organization's mission is "to lead, mobilize and engage professionals in pro bono service that drives social change." Generating $128 million in pro bono services for nonprofits, Taproot now has offices in Chicago, Los Angeles, New York City, San Francisco Bay Area, and Washington, D.C. Taproot Foundation's Advisory Services Practice offers consulting services to Fortune 100 companies, providing assistance in building high-impact pro bono programs.

And then there's Catchafire. Based in New York City, Catchafire is a for-purpose, social-mission business; a certified B-corporation; and a community of individuals striving to push the social-good sector forward by focusing on efficient and effective ways to give. The organization's primary activity is matching professionals with nonprofits on a project basis, based on their skills, interest, and time availability. Catchafire says that it is focused on "providing transformational volunteer experiences, so all of the nonprofits we welcome into our community must have demonstrable impact, strong leadership, and be aligned to our mission." Its services are not entirely free of charge; nonprofits are required to make a financial investment to confirm their commitment to their partnership and Catchafire consultants' time. This is how Catchafire describes their goal: "Our goal is to provide a significant return on investment for our partners and save them time, money and resources in finding talented and passionate individuals who have the potential to become long term advocates."

These are just two examples of organizations that are in the pro bono world. There are many more service firms, such as law, accounting, retired-executive organizations, and so on, that offer subject-matter expertise and time to nonprofit organizations. This is critical for nonprofits that need—but don't have the budget for—many services.

THE BOARD

Last but not least, we come to the primary subject of this book: the board of directors. The average size of a nonprofit board is sixteen individuals. Normally, the number of directors a board can have is set out in the organization's bylaws and is expressed as a range (for example, 16–20), rather than an exact number. Some organizations have term limits specifying how long an individual can remain a member of the board, while others allow board members to serve as long as they are able.

Board members may be called "super-volunteers" because they're just like any other volunteers, but with one important distinction: board members have the power to vote and, as a group, to take significant actions that affect the very essence of the organization.

In general terms, the board acts as trustee of the organization's assets and ensures that the nonprofit is properly managed and remains fiscally sound. To accomplish this, the board must exercise proper oversight of the organization's operations and maintain the legal and ethical accountability of its staff and volunteers.

Earlier we touched on a few of the responsibilities of nonprofit boards. Here is a more comprehensive list:

• Upholding and amending, as needed, the mission statement and bylaws

• Hiring, supporting, evaluating, and if necessary firing the executive director

• Providing proper financial oversight, including putting together and approving the annual budget, regularly reviewing financial reports, ensuring financial controls, and acting as stewards of the endowment and other assets

• Ensuring adequate resources for the organization to fulfill its mission by fundraising

• Adhering to legal standards and ethical norms

- Participating in an overall planning process and assisting in the implementation and monitoring of the organization's strategic plan

- Determining which programs are consistent with the organization's mission and monitoring their effectiveness

- Evaluating the board structure and functioning and developing the board to effectively meet the organization's needs through new members and training

The first step towards creating a strong and engaged board is for each member to have a clear expectation of what board service means both to nonprofits in general and to the specific organization that is being served. Board members should know what is expected of them. They should be provided with written roles and responsibilities, which may be delineated in a board members' handbook or manual. Some organizations ask board members to sign a contract or commitment letter acknowledging that they understand their roles and responsibilities. There are many versions of board commitment letters. For a sample Board Commitment Letter, please go to my website www.fridmanstrategies.com and use the password: **ONBOARD** to access the private download area.

Now that you know the general structure of a nonprofit, you are ready for the next question: "Is this organization a good fit for my talents, aspirations and life?" O

3

....

ENSURING THE ORGANIZATION
IS A GOOD FIT FOR YOU

*The way you get meaning into your life is to devote yourself
to loving others, devote yourself to your community around you,
and devote yourself to creating something that gives you
purpose and meaning.*

~ MITCH ALBOM, AUTHOR OF *TUESDAYS WITH MORRIE*

After you've received the phone call inviting you to join the board of the Sunrise Charitable Foundation, you may be ready to say "yes" because you've been volunteering there for years, and stepping up to the board seems like a natural progression. But let's say that your involvement has been more limited; you may know where the nonprofit is located and what they do, but you're not familiar with the inner workings. You don't know everyone on the current board and you don't know any of the professionals.

Because there are only so many hours in the day, you want to commit your time and money to a place where you'll be fulfilled and where your contribution will make a difference. You will need to determine if this organization and its mission are a match to the change agent aspect of *you*.

However, you will have to make a decision quickly! When your friend invites you to join the board, you owe the organization the courtesy of a prompt reply so that if necessary they can cross you off the list and ask someone else who may be interested. No one wants to be called and invited to join a board only to be told, "By the way, the first meeting is tomorrow. What's your answer?" If this happens, the invitee gets one of two messages, both bad: One, "You were last on our list," which is offensive; or two, "We are completely disorganized," which is depressing.

This should never happen. Ever.

Let's say that you need some time to learn more about the organization and about board service. If you are invited to join and the first meeting is in a month, you need to get motivated. It would be great if you could give an answer within a week so you don't leave the leadership development committee—and your friend—dangling.

Joining a board is a personal choice; no one can make the decision for you. Below are important questions that may be useful for you to ask, both of yourself and of the organization. Sometimes the board will interview prospective board members or provide a board job description; in other scenarios the prospective board member must take the lead role in getting the information needed to make an informed decision. You can download the following list of questions (without the commentary) at http://www.fridmanstrategies.com (password: **ONBOARD**). This list is ideal to use when researching the nonprofit and will help you in your personal consideration.

Board members who are interviewing prospective candidates can use these questions to guide your interviews and remind you of the topics you need to discuss. This will ensure that board members join with intentionality, clarity, and clear expectations—the best way to start off productive board service.

Do You Know Enough about the Organization and Does Its Work Speak to Your Heart?

• *Does the mission speak to you?*

Whether it's art, health, spirituality, education, or something else, the mission needs to be something in which you have both some experience and an interest. Remember, this is not a paid corporate-board position, where it is common for board members of a company to represent other industries; this is an organization to which you are donating your time and probably your money, too.

• *Do you share the vision of the organization?*

Nonprofits exist to affect change in the world. If you want to be an effective board member, you must share the organization's vision of a better world.

• *Have you toured the organization?*

It may be fairly easy to get acquainted with the physical resources of a small nonprofit that may occupy an office and storefront. But if you've been asked to join the board of a major museum or hospital, there may be entire areas of the operation that you have never seen. The professionals will appreciate meeting you too; in some organizations, board members are treated as if they were visiting royalty with whom no mere mortal should interact. You want to break these artificial barriers.

• *Are you familiar with the programs or services?*

Whether the organization provides cultural or educational programs, distributes food, or delivers services for the elderly, you should see it in action. This is where the rubber meets the road, so to speak, and it is good to have a working knowledge of how they operate.

• *Have you met those served?*

The whole point of a nonprofit is to improve the lives of its constituents. Having first-hand contact will give the mission of the organization a deeper meaning for you.

- *Do you care about this organization beyond "What's in it for me?"*

Will you be able to approach decision making with the organization's holistic best interest at heart as opposed to looking through your own lens to a particular program/staff/segment? You may have an interest in the organization because of a particular area of its activities; say it's an art museum, and you really enjoy contemporary fabric sculpture, which the museum has in its collections. You need to be able to see the big picture and not just advocate for the fabric sculpture exhibits. In other words, can you think organizationally?

Does Serving on This Particular Board Feel Exciting?

- *Have you met the other board members?*

This is very important. Your fellow board members are people with whom you will need to work closely. And remember, you are not getting paid. If your board service is not enjoyable, it will be drudgery, and you may even bail out early. On the other hand, if you personally like the people sitting with you at the table, the experience will be more fun and more rewarding. Generally, you would not have been asked to join if one or more current board members didn't already know you. This contact should informally bring you to a few events so that you can meet other board members in a no-pressure environment. If you decide is not what you want, no one need be uncomfortable.

- *How big is the board? Who is the current or incoming chair? What is the committee structure?*

These may sound like basic questions, but you'd be surprised how many potential board members don't know and don't bother to find out the answers until they show up for the first meeting. You're joining a team, and you owe it to yourself to get the answers. Also, I'm sure you'll agree that it would be embarrassing to come to the first meeting and have to ask,

"Who's in charge?" You'll be much more confident if you've learned these basic facts well ahead of time.

• *Will your skills and talents be leveraged by the board? How?*

This is also very important. In fact, the chances are good that you were asked to join the board because you would bring a set of skills or talents to the table that might be needed. Perhaps you are a lawyer who has been asked to join the board of the art museum. After speaking with the board chair, you learn that of the sixteen board members currently serving, none are lawyers. You also learn that the organization is planning a major new gallery construction project. You can be certain that your legal expertise will be called upon! Alternatively, if you learn that the board of the art museum already includes several lawyers, you might rightly wonder, "Why are they asking me?" It may be because of your network and fundraising ability. Don't be afraid to ask why the leadership development committee thought you would be a good addition if you need clarity. It's always more satisfying to serve on a board when you can add value.

Can You—and Do You *Want* to—Fulfill What Is Expected of You as a Board Member of This Organization?

• *What are board members' roles and responsibilities?*

Another key question. You need to know what you are getting into. At the very minimum you will be expected to attend the regular board meetings—once a month or perhaps quarterly—and often board members are expected to serve on at least once committee. But if that is all you think you need to do, you may be in for a surprise. This is a volunteer job, and it is going to be a good fit only if you have a passion for the mission of the organization. There will almost certainly be additional volunteer opportunities—special events, programs, and projects. Hopefully you will learn about areas where you are confident you can contribute—not just with money, but also with your time.

- *Do you have a policy of "give, get, or get off?"*

   Unless you're clear about the organization's expectations, you may be headed for major embarrassment. "Give" means the minimum donation of cash or securities that you are expected to make each year, generally to the annual fund. As I discussed earlier in the book, this may range from a token gift so that the community organization can report that 100 percent of the board has contributed in a given year to the seven-figure sums required by high-profile blue-chip organizations. "Get" means that if you cannot write the check yourself, you can get it from somewhere else. Board members who are executives often work for companies that allow the employee to make a donation to the charity of their choice using company funds. The funds come from the company and the company gets the tax deduction, but the employee gets the credit. Everyone goes home a winner. In other cases, board members control donor-advised charitable funds or have relatives or friends whom they can cultivate and induce to write checks for the organization. "Get off" is often left unspoken, but it is implied. It means just what it says: If you don't pony up, at the end of the year the board chair will take you aside and discreetly suggest that maybe the board hasn't been a good fit for you and that perhaps a year off is a good idea.

- *Do you feel like you want to give money to this organization?*

   Or, more accurately, are you comfortable with making the minimum donation? Giving is an expression of values. You may wish to give much more than the required minimum, of course, but you do not want to suffer the embarrassment of not being able to donate at the minimal level to the annual fund or capital campaign.

- *Are you willing to ask others to give money to this organization?*

   Don't worry—not everyone is comfortable doing this. If you can ask, fine. If you cannot, then the executive director or development person can approach your contacts whom you think have the capability and interest.

- *Do you feel like you could be an ambassador for the organization and its mission?*

When you go to community events or business networking events, you need to be comfortable being identified as a board member. People may ask you about the organization, and they may be considering making a gift or attending a special event. (This will be discussed in a later chapter, "Being an Ambassador and a Friendraiser.")

- *Does serving on this board pose any conflict of interests for you?*

It is unlikely, but it is possible, particularly if your company has business dealings with the nonprofit.

- *What training do new board members receive?*

Is there an information packet or binder for new members? Is there an informal get-together where you can meet other board members and get a feeling for what they do? Or perhaps there is a formal orientation process where you will be provided with an in-depth preview of what the organization expects from you and how you will be asked to contribute.

Do the Time, Timing, and Logistics of Serving Work for You?

- *How long is the term, and do you have term limits?*

Basic stuff, but you should ask about this because every organization is different. While some nonprofits allow—and even encourage—board members to be "lifers," who serve for years and even decades, the trend is to have term limits because the organization wants fresh faces on a regular basis. Boards are generally reconstituted once a year, but your organization may be the exception.

- *What is the time commitment for board members?*

Once you determine that you are indeed interested in serving the organization because of the work it does, it is time to figure out if your busy life allows for you to meet the board's requirements and responsibilities. For example, a board that meets quarterly may be manageable, but a board that meets monthly may be too much. In addition to meetings and special events, board members often have other responsibilities. If your social-service agency requires board members to also be a big buddy and have weekly contact and monthly outings with your little buddy, is that something you have time to do? Along the same lines, if your religious organization's board members are required to attend religious services monthly, is that something to which you can commit?

- *How often and when does the board meet?*

An obvious question, but you'd be surprised how many board members don't bother to find out. Board meetings are typically once a month or quarterly, either on a regular basis or a less predictable schedule, and there are also committee meetings and special events. A responsible board member (that person being you) will look at the calendar once you know the dates and give notice about when you cannot attend. "My family will be on vacation during the week of the July board meeting," you might say. "Also, I'll be away on business in October and January, so I'll miss three meetings out of twelve. Is that okay?" This might be okay, especially if the big fundraising gala—which you have volunteered to co-chair—is held in April of each year. "No problem," you say. "I'll be 100 percent committed!" If you miss a few board meetings, no one will mind as long as you keep up to date with the board minutes and you're actively involved in other areas.

- *In general, how long are meetings?*

Another no-brainer question, but one worth asking, especially if travel time is a consideration. No one wants a board meeting to drag on until ten o'clock at night when facing an hour's drive home. This is where you will quickly learn to appreciate having an effective board chairperson. It is his or her responsibility to keep board meetings on the agenda, moving forward and on schedule.

- *Can I participate via tele- or video conference during meetings?*

If you travel a lot, this may be a question worth asking, especially if you want to participate in a key meeting.

• *Are there any board retreats or other special sessions?*

Some organizations have annual weekend retreats at which board members are immersed in training and team-building sessions. It's a good idea to inquire about any board events that are scheduled in addition to the regular meetings.

One way to have all these questions answered (besides the personal ones, which you will need to ask yourself) is to meet with either the leadership development committee or the board chair. Come to the meeting armed with your questions. Don't be shy about this; the current board members don't want a bad fit any more than you do. The last thing they want is an unhappy board member who doesn't contribute because it is not what he or she expected or because the new member was cajoled into joining and really did not want to be there. It is also helpful to meet with the executive director. He or she can give a different perspective of board involvement and engagement.

The leadership development committee is important when you are seeking information about logistics of board service. In some cases, you will be provided with information about the organization and expectations of board members at the time you are offered a seat on the board.

The bottom line is that if you need to get more information about serving on the board before you accept, you should be proactive. Pick up the phone, ask for a meeting, and get the answers that you need to make an informed decision.

Reach out to the person who has issued the invitation to you, and inquire. You can also ask to meet other board members. The more you know, the better equipped you will be to evaluate if serving on the board at this time makes sense and, if you chose to accept, to become an effective board member.

Serving on a nonprofit board should be rewarding and even fun. By doing your due diligence, you will have a good idea whether or not you will be a good fit on the board—and whether serving on the board will be a good fit for you.

ABOUT THE LEADERSHIP DEVELOPMENT COMMITTEE (FORMERLY REFERRED TO AS THE NOMINATING COMMITTEE)

During the phone call from your friend who serves on the board of the Sunrise Charitable Foundation, he or she mentioned that in a month the organization will install the board for the upcoming year. This is something that is done every year, and each year some board members stay on while others leave and need to be replaced. Let's say that of the sixteen Sunrise board members, twelve are staying for another year while four are rolling off and need to be replaced.

The three members of the board's leadership development committee have been charged with identifying and contacting potential board members. ("Leadership development committee" is the more current best-practice name for the "nominating committee"; it reflects the committee's broader responsibilities of training and succession planning rather than simply asking people to join the board.) This doesn't mean that the three volunteers—your friend is one of them— are personally responsible for knowing and recruiting every new board member. This would be an unfair burden. It is the responsibility of all board members, the executive director, and even senior staff members to offer names of potential board members. The leadership development committee's function is to keep the effort organized and to act as the official representatives of the board to the candidates. This can be an extremely sensitive job. An organization cannot have a multitude of well-meaning people running around town offering spots on the board to their friends. The effort needs to be tightly controlled.

In order to make the process of identification and assessment more scientific, some larger nonprofits keep a matrix or chart delineating two sets of data: the skills that are desirable in their board members and the actual skills of board members who are currently serving. If you have skills that are needed but are currently underrepresented, your chances of being asked will increase. For example, if you are a practicing real-estate attorney and a board member who is also a real-estate attorney is rotating off, thereby leaving a void, your value to the organization will increase. Other key factors in selection of members include business and social networks, diversity, and geographical location.

The one ironclad rule of the leadership development committee is that you never, ever officially ask individuals to join the board unless you really truly want them and you have a very good reason to believe that they will accept the offer. An invitation to join cannot be retracted. ○

4

··

LEGAL DUTIES AND DUE DILIGENCE

Rank does not confer privilege or give power.
It imposes responsibility.

~ PETER DRUCKER

DUTIES AND POTENTIAL LIABILITIES

As mentioned earlier, serving as a board member is like being a super-volunteer with one big difference: collectively, the board is required to cast votes on matters that impact people's lives, such as budgets, whether to keep or fire the executive director, program or event approvals, campaigns, and so on. These all can have an impact on the lives of real people and their families.

Before we discuss the general principles of the legal landscape, I want to be clear that this book does not dispense legal advice nor offer an opinion on how a law may apply to your particular situation. If you have specific legal questions, you should seek legal counsel.

That being said, let's review some basic principles and definitions of board members' obligations under the applicable laws in the United States. A person who has a relationship of trust or confidence with another is called a *fiduciary*. A fiduciary's relationship with an organization is one-sided, which means that the relationship serves to meet the needs of the organization alone. The fiduciary (in this case, the board member) must act without regard to his or her needs. The fiduciary must be concerned only about the performance of the nonprofit and must make every effort to ensure that its interests are pursued faithfully.

The primary legal responsibilities of a nonprofit board are often summarized in the "three Ds": Duty of Care, Duty of Loyalty, and Duty of Obedience.

Duty of Care

Board members are expected to actively participate in organizational planning and decision making and to make sound and informed judgments. For example, when making a decision, board members may need the professional staff to provide appropriate information. If board members find that the information is inaccurate or incomplete, they need to ask questions and determine why. If the nonprofit is considering a major initiative, such as buying or selling significant assets, conducting a capital campaign, or entering into a material contract, qualified independent advice is required.

Duty of Loyalty

When acting on behalf of the organization, board members must put the interests of the nonprofit before any personal or professional concerns and avoid potential conflicts of interest. A board member cannot advocate an opportunity for his or her own personal gain. Similarly, it is a breach of the duty of loyalty to fail to preserve the confidentiality of the organization's affairs. Disclosing opportunities to outside individuals may lead to loss of opportunity for the organization.

Duty of Obedience

Board members must ensure that the organization complies with all applicable federal, state, and local laws and regulations and that it remains committed to its established mission.

Compliance with these obligations provides protection for a nonprofit board and its members. As long as decisions of the directors are made on an informed and independent basis, in good faith, and in the best interests of the organization, they are not subject to challenge in court. This presumption is called "the business judgment rule" and applies unless evidence is presented showing a board member has an interest in the transaction or dispute or was uninformed, disloyal, or lacking in independence.

As a volunteer, you'll be working without a legally binding contract (although you may have a good faith agreement or commitment letter). You have the legal right at any time to simply walk away by resigning before your term ends. (Of course, you'd never do this—but it underscores the idea that good faith is the bedrock upon which every board relationship is built.) Thus, the normal avenues of dispute that are settled by contract law do not exist. Although the law recognizes that fiduciary relationships on nonprofit boards tend to occur outside of a contractual relationship, fiduciaries still need to be held to high standards.

Board members have an obligation to monitor and oversee not only the organization's financial affairs but also its ongoing regulatory compliance program. For most nonprofit, non-religious organizations this includes the annual audit and the filing of the IRS Form 990. In nonprofit hospitals and health-care organizations, failure to comply with patient privacy regulations, fraud and abuse statutes, and other federal and state laws can expose a hospital or system to significant criminal and civil penalties that could impact its ability to provide care. Health care organizations may be excluded from participation in Medicare, Medicaid, and other federal health-care programs; such exclusion and the loss of reimbursement payments can spell the end of a hospital or system.

In matters of budget and finance, while every board member cannot be a financial expert, every board member—including those who are focused on non-financial vocations, such as art or human services—needs to understand basic terminology, to be able to read financial statements, and to be able to perceive the warning signs that indicate a financial problem. If a board member does not understand something, he or she must be willing to find out the answer.

In Chapter 15, which deals with crises and challenges, I will discuss in greater depth the pitfalls to be avoided by boards. For now, I want to point out that nonprofit boards open themselves to charges of breached duties not only when there is malfeasance or bad actions, such as a breach of confidentiality, but more often when the board commits nonfeasance by being asleep at the wheel.

One of my clients did not have accurately balanced books for a period of twenty years. I learned this when I came in to help with a strategic plan. The lack of financial control and oversight was shocking! It not only made the board look unprofessional but also inhibited their ability to raise funds from donors, who feared they would be "throwing good money after bad." In addition, they (and the prior boards) were breaching their fiduciary duties. How could they know the true financial status of the organization if they didn't have real numbers? This put the organization in real jeopardy. Needless to say, putting proper financial controls, procedures, and knowledgeable staff and board oversight in place was primary for this organization.

To keep your board on secure footing, you and every board member need to clearly understand and carry out your legal responsibilities to the best of your abilities.

Avoiding Liability

As board members, you can meet your obligations and avoid liability by taking the following actions.

1. *Attend meetings and be informed.* Being present at most meetings is important to fulfill your duty of care. Of course, all board members need to miss occasional meetings, but be sure to review the minutes and talk to the board chair or CEO about key information discussed at the meeting. Make sure that you receive detailed information beforehand about those matters to be voted on at a meeting.

2. *Keep the organization true to its mission.* It is important as board members that you hold the nonprofit to its stated mission or its charitable status could be jeopardized. If the mission starts to creep or resources are being allocated to programs or services not in line with the organization's mission, as board members you need to call for a mission check. To ensure the charitable purpose, individual board members should be provided with copies of the organization's mission statement, strategic plan, annual budget, and an overview of programs and staff.

3. *Establish key committees.* As I'll discuss in greater depth later in the book, most of the day-to-day work of a board is done by its various committees. This is because committees that are composed of three or four board members are much more able to focus on a single issue, bring the members' expertise to bear, and either act independently or swiftly create a set of recommendations on which the board can vote. Committees meet as needed—some, such as special events committees, multiple times during the week leading up to the event—and utilize the services of relevant members of the professional staff, outside consultants, and volunteers. In contrast, there is no way that a twenty-five-member board can possibly address in detail every important issue.

4. *Establish a mechanism for board review.* The board should conduct an annual self-evaluation. It may use the metrics established by its strategic plan as a measure of success and also look to comparable organizations or survey the organization's staff to determine additional measures.

5. *Adopt appropriate ethics policies.* In the course of fulfilling their duties on the board, directors must keep the confidences of the organization and act at all times in its best interests and not for personal or third-party gain or financial enrichment. For example, it would be improper for a board member to sell services to the nonprofit, such as accounting, catering, computer, or construction and earn a profit. It would also be

inappropriate for a board member to try to influence the staff to award a consulting contract to a friend or business associate.

A written conflict-of-interest policy will outline those relationships and dealings that may pose an ethical or legal problem for the board member or the organization. The policy may also state the conditions under which it would be acceptable to conduct business with an entity with which there is a conflict. Best practice is for board members to sign a disclosure form every year that identifies potential conflicts. A confidentiality policy spells out how to define what matters are confidential and when or if to make statements to the press or public.

If a conflict of interest arises, the board member should make a full disclosure of the conflict to the rest of the board. Unless he or she is in a position to impart information that will help board members who are not conflicted to reach a decision, the board member should withdraw from any discussion concerning the transaction and must always abstain from voting on the issue.

A code of conduct may include a commitment to ethics and compliance, standards for business practices, standards of conduct, and standards for employees.

6. *Understand and comply with workplace rules and local, state, and federal rules and regulations to fulfill the duty of obedience.* While such compliance is most often the direct responsibility of the executive director or CEO, as a board member you need to have an awareness of employment and financial reporting regulations; the rules regarding tax-exempt gifts; and in hospitals and other organizations that provide human services, appropriate standards of care. Remember, it is your job to evaluate the performance of the professional management of the organization.

7. *Use your own judgment.* Do not simply take the word of the CEO or fellow board members. Understand the agency, its activities, and the issues at hand and ask any and all questions. Make sure you have enough information when asked to make a decision.

Immunity, Indemnification, and Insurance

Most states have adopted some form of *charitable immunity* statutes providing individuals who serve as officers and directors on nonprofit boards with limited liability to third parties. Exoneration statutes do not prohibit suits resulting from gross negligence or actions intended to result in harm to the claimant and may not apply to causes of action arising under federal law. For example, the Internal Revenue Code creates a presumptive liability of a director or officer for unpaid withholding taxes of employees.

Further, nonprofits customarily indemnify directors from liability in their bylaws and sometimes their articles of organization. In addition to statutory protection and indemnification, nonprofits, like for-profits, can purchase directors' and officers' liability insurance, sometimes referred to as *D&O insurance*. Policies generally protect against breach of a duty owed to the organization by a director or an officer, but they differ greatly; therefore, you will want to ask for a copy of the specific policy in effect as part of your due diligence.

DUE DILIGENCE

In Chapter 3, I put forth a set of questions to help you determine if the organization's mission and work speak to you enough to devote your time, energy, and financial resources to further its cause. If you decide that you are interested and able to join the board, you will want to learn more about the substance and operations of the organization. Your due diligence will pay off in one of two ways: you will either discover that you do not really want to get involved with this organization; or, more happily, that your understanding of the operational nuts and bolts of the nonprofit and its board will make you a more effective and responsible board member.

Being a board member means that you are a non-compensated volunteer who, together with your colleagues on the board, have the voting power to impact peoples' lives. You hire, evaluate, and if necessary fire the executive director. You approve the annual budget, which in difficult economic times may result in budget cuts and, therefore, layoffs. You vote on major projects, such as building a new wing or a gallery. All of these decisions must be made thoughtfully and with a sense of responsibility.

In the pages that follow, I discuss the key documents, reports, and information that you should ask to see before, or in some cases, shortly after accepting a place on the board. Frequently, these materials will be given out during a board orientation or first meeting. For my clients, I recommend that board members be given binders that consist of these key organizational documents and training materials and that provide ample space for future agendas and meeting notes. If you don't get an organized binder or folder from the nonprofit, I suggest making one for yourself.

This information is also useful for anyone who is currently serving on a board and has unanswered questions (this is not uncommon!). In a 501(c)(3) nonprofit, much of the information described below may be available on the organization's website because many organizations believe that transparency is important for attracting donors and supporters. If you don't see it, you can ask your board contact, finance-committee chair, board chair, or executive director.

Most tax-exempt organizations that have gross receipts of at least $200,000 or assets worth at least $500,000 must file a Form 990 with the Internal Revenue Service every year. (As discussed earlier, some organizations, such as political organizations, churches, and other religious organizations, are exempt from filing an annual Form 990.) The Form 990s are public records. The form gives the IRS—and anyone who reads it—an overview of the organization's activities, governance, and detailed financial information. Form 990 also includes a section for the organization to outline its accomplishments in the previous year to justify maintaining its tax-exempt status. In collecting this information, the IRS wants to ensure that organizations continue to qualify for tax exemption after the status is granted.

If for some reason the Form 990 of the organization is not immediately available, you can download it from GuideStar.org. Founded in Williamsburg, Virginia, in September 1994, GuideStar is the first and the largest central source of online information on nonprofits in the United States. In 2010, their database contained over 5 million IRS Forms 990 on 1.9 million organizations.

Here are the key documents that you should review. If the organization does not have any or all of the following items, this should be a red flag, and I would ask the board chair or executive director to explain.

The Mission and Vision Statements

As I discussed in Chapter 2, the mission statement, along with any additional formulations, such as a vision or values statement, describes the fundamental essence of what the organization is trying to accomplish. These statements need to be in alignment with your personal interests and aspirations.

The Strategic Plan

Every organization, whether for-profit or nonprofit, should have a strategic plan. Strategic planning engages the staff and board in defining strategy and approving both priorities and measurable objectives. At the end of the planning process, usually a document called a strategic plan is produced and approved by the board. A strategic plan, or implementation plan, outlines in detail the operational steps that will be taken in the over a period of time, usually two to five years, to fulfill the organization's mission. I cannot overestimate the importance of having a strategic plan. We will review it in more detail in Chapter 9.

Audited Financials

These are the formal financial statements that are annually created by an independent accountant. You may see that your nonprofit operates on a fiscal year that does not correspond to the calendar year (for example, July 1st to June 30th is one fiscal year). This may be because the nonprofit operates on a seasonal cycle or simply because the accounting firm offers a lower price to clients whose fiscal years begin and end during slower months. Financial statements are important not only for the expected ethical reasons but also because grant-making foundations often want to see them. They can reveal things like whether the organization has been operating at a deficit and the value of its endowment. Audited financials will be part of the Form 990 filing.

Balance Sheet

Also called a statement of financial position, this is a summary of the financial balances of the organization. Assets and liabilities are listed as of a specific date, such as the end of the fiscal year. A balance sheet is often described as a snapshot of the organization's financial condition. Of the three basic financial statements—balance sheet, statement of cash flows, and income statement—the balance sheet is the only one that applies to a single point in time of the organization's calendar year. Balance sheets are usually presented with three parts: assets; liabilities; and net worth, or net assets, which is the difference between the assets and liabilities.

In the section that presents the difference between the total assets and total liabilities, the nonprofit's statement of financial position refers to this section as net assets, whereas the for-profit business will refer to this section as owner's equity or stockholders' equity. The reason for this difference is that the nonprofit does not have owners.

The net assets section will consist of the following parts: unrestricted net assets, temporarily restricted net assets, and permanently restricted net assets. The amounts reported in each of these parts are based on the donors' stipulations.

Cash Flows Statement

The statement of cash flows for a nonprofit organization is similar to that of a for-profit business. It reports the organization's change in its cash and cash equivalents during the specified accounting period. The statement of cash flows consists of three sections:

1. Net cash from operating activities, which reports the changes in cash other than those reported in the investing and financing sections

2. Net cash from investing activities, which reports the amounts spent to purchase long-term assets, such as vehicles, equipment, and long-term investments, as well as income received from the sale of said assets

3. Net cash from financing activities, which reports the amounts received from borrowings and also any repayments

Note: In the private-access area on our website is a special download called Glossary of Financial Terms to help it all make sense. Go to www.fridmanstrategies.com and enter the password: **ONBOARD.**

Year-To-Date Budget

The annual budget is approved before the start of the new fiscal year, but it isn't set in stone. It is reviewed periodically; any variances from target goals are noted; and if necessary, action is taken. For example, if the annual fund is 10 percent under its year-to-date target, the board should know this and have the opportunity either to take action (raise more money or cut expenses) or to adopt a wait-and-see position.

The Organization's Bylaws

The bylaws are the organization's operating manual, and collectively they govern the organization's internal operations. They address these matters:

- Size of the board and how it will function

- Responsibilities of directors and officers

- Conflict-of-interest policies and procedures

- Policies and procedures for holding meetings, electing board members, and appointing board officers

State nonprofit laws usually address nonprofit governance matters. Bylaws are not required to be public documents, but making them available increases the organization's accountability and transparency and encourages the board to act responsibly. A well-planned and clear set of bylaws will reduce the potential for conflict within the organization, especially in the event of disagreement between board members.

Organizational Chart

In a small community nonprofit, there may not be one. But in a large organization with multiple departments and lots of employees, seeing the organizational chart will give you a good idea of how the nonprofit works. You may spot departments or divisions that you don't know much about and consequently choose to visit.

History of the Organization

It's nice to know how the nonprofit got started and the big picture of how it has grown. It is also wise to be familiar with the older generation of big donors and board leaders; frequently these founding or wealthy donors will make a sizable gift or bequest to the organization, and you should be up to speed on who these people are.

Indemnification Provisions and Directors' and Officers' Liability Insurance Policies

Beyond clearly understanding your duties and carrying them out to the best of your ability, directors have further protection from liability. To understand the protection offered, the organization should provide to directors a summary of applicable state laws, indemnification provisions in the organization's articles of organization or bylaws, and the specific terms of the D&O insurance. If so desired, a director should obtain competent legal and insurance advice to fully understand any remaining potential liability resulting from his or her service on the board.

The Organization in Action

In addition to all the documents listed, if you haven't already witnessed the organization in action, the best way to learn about the organization's people and services or programs is to conduct a site visit. If you are asked to join a group that provides after-school programs, try to arrange a time through your board contact to visit the school or community center site during after-school hours. If you are joining a food bank, you may want to observe during food distribution. Seeing the service in action coupled with understanding the governance structure, business model, and financials of the nonprofit will ensure you are well informed and ready to join and contribute to the organization's board of directors.

Something that is harder to learn from a document is the culture of an organization. Organizational culture, or corporate culture, is an overarching term that outlines the collective attitudes, beliefs, values, norms, systems, and procedures that are prevalent in an organization and others similar to it. It is the way the people behave and interact. Asking about the culture will give you insight into the workplace.

Understanding your duties and completing your due diligence will give you a strong understanding of your role and the structure, financials, and plans of the nonprofit board on which you have been asked to serve. In the following chapters I'll discuss in greater depth the inner workings of the nonprofit board and your role in it. ○

5

HOW YOUR BOARD WORKS

Never doubt that a small group of thoughtful, committed citizens can change the world. Indeed, it is the only thing that ever has.

~ MARGARET MEAD

Congratulations! You've decided to join, and you are attending your first meeting as a member of the Sunshine Charitable Foundation board of directors. With a sense of excitement and anticipation, you make your way into the meeting room. If it is a big organization, you may find yourself in a dedicated boardroom with a long wooden table ringed by leather-covered chairs. If it is a small community organization, you might find your seat at one of the sixteen folding chairs set up around a couple of banquet tables that are stored in the utility closet for use at events. Either way, you've done your due diligence and you feel confident that together with your colleagues on the board, you'll be able to guide the organization through another successful year and help position it for future success.

You may be wondering how the board is structured, how meetings are run, how people are sorted into committees, and what the rules of discussion are. Keep reading!

OFFICERS

Generally, a board consists of a number of regular members and four or more officers. The officers are elected by the board to serve terms of one or more years articulated in the bylaws of the organization. These officers include the following:

President or Chair

This person presides at board meetings, ensures the effective action of the board in governing and supporting the organization, and oversees board affairs. Together with the executive director, the chair develops the agenda in preparation of board meetings.

The chair appoints all committee chairs and with the executive director seeks volunteers for committees and coordinates individual board-member committee assignments. He or she determines whether executive committee meetings are necessary and convenes the committee accordingly.

When time comes to hire a new executive director, the chair establishes the search and selection committee. The chair also convenes committee discussions on evaluating the executive director and negotiating the director's compensation and liaises with the executive director.

Vice President or Vice-Chair

This individual fulfills the immediate duties of the chair in his or her absence and assists the chair with the above or other specified duties. This person may be in line to succeed the outgoing chair. It is not uncommon to have more than one vice president to facilitate succession planning.

Treasurer

This person manages the board's financial responsibilities and makes regular financial reports to the board. The treasurer works directly with the accountant or other staff in developing and implementing financial procedures and systems.

Secretary

This member is responsible for proper management of important records, such as the organization's bylaws, and for creating the meeting minutes. He or she provides proper notice of meetings and ensures the timely distribution of agendas, meeting minutes, and other materials. To facilitate communication, some nonprofits have secure sections of their websites for board members to log in.

Committee Chairs

These individuals are generally not formally elected. They volunteer or are asked, and the board chair confirms their positions. They are responsible for the work of their committees and for making reports to the board prior to or during meetings.

Ex Officio Board or Committee Members

You may have heard this term and wondered what it means. Don't worry; most people don't know!

An *ex officio* member is a member of a body (a board, committee, or council) who is part of it by virtue of holding another office, either within or outside the organization. The term is Latin, meaning literally "from the office," and the sense intended is "by right of office." Its use dates back to the Roman Republic.

Ex officio defines a method of sitting on a committee, not a class of membership. While ex officio members sometimes abstain from voting, unless the bylaws formally constrain their rights, they are afforded the same rights as other members, including the right to debate, to make formal motions, and to vote.

Who is an ex officio member? Typically, any ex officio membership (for example, of committees, or of the board) will be as defined by the nonprofit's bylaws, which may provide, for example, that the organization's president will be ex officio a member of all board committees except the leadership development committee.

Ex officio members might also be people who are not members of the organization but who hold some outside position of relevance to the board or committee. For example, an independent financial advisor may be an ex officio member of the organization's finance committee without having any further involvement with the board or the organization.

Executive Director or CEO

In most nonprofit boards, the executive director is a permanent board member. His or her influence over the board can vary tremendously. In some organizations, the board serves as a volunteer body that follows the executive director's lead; in others, the executive director is a manager, who takes his or her marching orders from the board and is the direct report for all staff. I will discuss the dynamic of the executive director and the board in detail in Chapter 8.

Meeting Schedule

Most nonprofit boards meet either monthly or quarterly on a set day of the week, such as the second Tuesday of each month. Regular meetings are usually on weekdays either early for breakfast before work hours or after five pm, so that members can come to the meeting directly before or after work. Seasonal nonprofits, such as colleges or art associations, may skip one or more board meetings during the summer months. An efficiently run regular meeting should take no more than two hours. In addition to the regular meetings, the schedule for the board meeting may also include events such as these:

Orientation

This is an occasion for board veterans to meet and greet new members and for new members to receive their board information packets. Tours of the organization's facility may be included. The orientation may be informal or very structured.

Annual Meeting

An annual meeting is a big event that may include ancillary individuals, such as professional staff, members of the organization, and "friends-of" groups. This event may be preceded or followed by a social component such as a meal or cocktail reception. Once the meeting is convened, the chair and executive director (and possibly others) will present annual reports in a series of state-of-the-union messages and lay out the themes for the coming year. It is also a customary time to recognize volunteers and staff for exemplary service or milestones. Regular business typically does not take place except for one item that's very important: the vote on new board members and officers.

Annual or Semi-Annual Retreats

These events allow for more time to discuss issues in depth, such as the strategic plan or the launch of a campaign. The retreat may be very informal and last just one weekend afternoon, or it may be for an entire weekend at a resort or facility that specializes in hosting retreats. The agenda for a board retreat may include the following:

- Review of the prior year (financials and highlights, positives, negatives, lessons learned)

- A SWOT analysis (strengths, weaknesses, opportunities, threats) of the organization

- Objectives for the coming year or several years

Retreats are also an ideal time for the board to receive training.

Committee Meetings

Your board service will probably include participation in one or more committees (which I will discuss more in depth later in this chapter). Committee meetings happen as needed. While committees often meet either before or after the regular board meeting, many committees need to meet, in person or virtually, according to the demands of the project.

Training

Because fundraising is an important part of a board's portfolio and because this is precisely the activity that many board members find uncomfortable, many organizations sponsor board trainings. Professional fundraising consultants like me, who gently ease reluctant board members into the roles of fundraisers, often manage these types of trainings. These trainings are most common at the onset of major fundraising efforts such as major gifts, capital, or endowment campaigns. Other training sessions may focus on how to be a more effective and engaged board member.

Training is an investment that an organization makes in its people and its future. For example, when I trained a small cohort of board members on major-gifts fundraising, one of the women in the group, we'll call her Ava, approached me at the beginning and said that she was only at the training as a favor to the President but she would not be asking anyone for money. After our third session (spread over six weeks), we began to assign prospects to people who had been trained. Much to my surprise, Ava volunteered to meet with several important prospects. In fact, she was the first person to complete her meetings and report back on her progress. Why the change of heart? Because once Ava understood the campaign message, learned what to expect during a solicitation and role-played different scenarios while anticipating common questions and objections, she was comfortable and ready to meet with potential donors. Ava is not atypical. Fundraising is a skill. As with most skills, you need to learn the basics and some tricks of the trade and you must practice before you feel ready to try it out. Organizations get a good return on their investment with fundraising and other board trainings.

Special Events

While special events are not board meetings per se, most nonprofits expect board members to attend fundraising events, such as the annual gala or benefit auction. In addition, board members may be encouraged to attend other public events held by the nonprofit, such as art-exhibit openings or special services in a house of worship. It is considered to be good bridge building when staff and volunteers see board members at events, and it is also a primary way for members to cultivate new board prospects and donors.

THE FORMAT OF REGULAR MEETINGS

Most nonprofit board meetings are conducted according to the guidelines set forth in *Robert's Rules of Order*. This is the informal title of the book written by United States Brig. Gen. Henry Martyn Robert and published in 1876; it specifies those rules of order the author intended to be adopted for use by any deliberative assembly.

Robert's system helps move meetings from the introduction through the adjournment. It sets specific methods for making a motion, handling discussions, amending a motion, and calling a vote. The official rules are available for review on the Robert's Rules of Order website (www.robertsrules.com). While some organizations might not mandate the use of Robert's Rules in their bylaws and instead run a more informal meeting, most follow an organized agenda and use many of the elements of Robert's Rules for taking votes. If the organization uses another system, such as *The Standard Code of Parliamentary Procedure,* by Alice Sturgis, ask the secretary for a copy of those rules and familiarize yourself with them before your first meeting.

As a guideline for the meeting and to give participants a chance to prepare, nonprofit board meetings use an agenda prepared and distributed in advance along with any materials that board members might need to review before the meeting. This is a typical agenda:

- A call to order, made by the board chair

- Roll call, done by the secretary

- Introduction of any guests

- Approval of the minutes of the previous meeting

- Regular reports by the board chair, the treasurer or finance-committee chair, and the executive director

- Topics to be discussed and decisions to be made

- Committee reports (such as special events or development)

- New business (open to any board member to initiate)

- Old business

- Adjournment

Boards who want to make good use of their members' time are spending less time with staff and committee chairs talking *at* the board and more time having strategic discussions and learning from the experiences of the board members. This means putting information and reports that don't require discussion in writing and sending them out by e-mail ahead of time or distributing them at the meeting.

The secretary takes detailed minutes of the meeting; if the secretary is absent, another member needs to fill in. In some instances, organizations are doing away with the secretary position and a staff member takes the minutes at meetings.

When a new motion is to be considered, the chair calls for a member to submit the new motion. Then another member is asked to second the motion. Having done this, the chair opens the floor for discussion. This is when an effective chair is a huge asset. It is the chair's job to keep the discussion on topic and not let any member drone on about some arcane detail that should be settled away from the meeting. All of this must be done while creating the feeling that everyone's voice is heard and respected.

At such time as the chair deems the matter has been adequately discussed, it is put to a vote. The chair asks who is in favor of the motion, who is against it, and who abstains; he or she then announces whether the measure has passed or has been rejected.

The number of board members who must be present and able to vote is called the *quorum*. A quorum is necessary because, obviously, if only three members of a sixteen-member board show up at a meeting and vote, it's an empty exercise that has no legal authority. The number necessary for a quorum must be stated in the organization's bylaws. Generally it is half the total number of the board; for a sixteen-person board, it would be eight people. But it may be more or less depending upon the track record of the organization; if the total number on the board is twenty-five but never more than twenty active members ever show up at one time, a quorum may be fixed at ten.

TYPES OF COMMITTEES

I will discuss committee work in greater depth later in the book, but this is a great place to give you an overview of committee *types*.

As you can imagine, it is difficult and often pointless for large groups of people—such as an entire board of twenty or more people—to focus on every operational project. Specific tasks are better performed by smaller groups of specialists who can work together on their own time before bringing their results to the board. Committees are created for efficiency. If board members are enthusiastic volunteers, it is not uncommon to have many committees designed to complete necessary projects and to bring their ideas to the board for a full board vote. Staff members should be assigned to work with volunteers on each committee.

Permanent

Permanent committees, also called *standing* committees or *operating* committees, are those that are specified in the organization's bylaws; they may include executive, finance, development, operations, program, marketing/public relations, planning, nominating/leadership development, personnel, and audit committees as may be required. They tend to operate year round.

Ad-hoc

Ad hoc committees, also called special committees or task forces, are those that are not articulated in the bylaws but are formed by the board to achieve a specified task. When the work of the ad hoc committee is completed, the committee is dissolved. Depending on the extent of the work assigned to it, an ad hoc committee may exist for less than a year or for several years. Ad hoc or special committees are often formed for a one-time or seasonal project, such as to recruit a new CEO, to amend the organization's bylaws or mission statement, to develop a strategic plan, to relocate the organization, to launch a new venture or subsidiary, to create a new educational program, or work with other organizations or coalitions. An ad hoc committee might also be formed to research and propose solutions to a particular challenge faced by the organization, such as falling visitor numbers, declining membership levels, or a problem with one of the organization's buildings (the Leaky Roof Committee!). Other issues may include site relocation or capital campaign, coordinating a special event, undergoing CEO transitions and searches, pursuing a possible merger or strategic consolidation, and strategic planning endeavors. Ad hoc committees often involve non-board members in the work of the board, such as the roof contractor or executive recruiter.

Executive

An executive committee usually comprises the board officers plus one or two others. It is not supposed to be a surrogate board; it handles important issues between board meetings and sensitive issues that require discretion as necessary. It is a big red flag if the executive board decides everything and then expects the regular board members to "rubber stamp" their decisions. This used to happen when boards were very large, but over the last twenty years board sizes tend to have gotten smaller, so the board itself can exercise meaningful governance.

Finance

The finance committee is responsible for overseeing the budget process and monitoring expenditures. It ensures that audits are performed and IRS forms completed and submitted. Often, especially in light of Sarbanes-Oxley, a separate audit committee will exist to oversee the audit function.

Audit

The audit committee oversees the selection of auditors, receives the auditor's report, meets with the auditor, and responds to the auditor's recommendations.

Development

This committee is responsible for meeting budget demands by working with the professional staff to plan for and implement a financial resource development strategy. Revenue in the form of donations may be raised by annual appeal, grant writing, major gifts, endowment gifts, capital campaigns, planned giving, and special fundraising events.

Operations

Similar to an internal-affairs committee. The operations committee is most often seen in hospitals, universities, and other large organizations that have complex ongoing operations.

Programming

Most nonprofits have a schedule of programs that may include evening classes or lectures, weekend seminars, or summer camps for kids. The program committee works with the executive director and professional staff to develop and oversee educational and other outreach programs, to develop new programs, and to monitor and assess existing programs through evaluation.

Marketing/Public Relations

This type of committee ensures that the organization is well represented in the media and that the organization's services, programs, and events are advertised. If there is no professional marketing (PR staff), this committee will help with tasks like coordinating collateral design, forwarding good news, posting on social media, and monitoring Google alerts. It may also be involved with surveys or other efforts to assess the organization's place in the community.

Planning

The planning committee is accountable for strategic plan preparation, implementation tracking, and updating plans. May also spearhead capital-expansion plans.

Leadership Development/Nominating

In addition to being responsible for identifying, evaluating, and asking candidates to join the board, this committee is also responsible for board leadership development through training and mentoring and planning for succession.

Human Resources/Personnel

The personnel committee is in charge of drafting and/or revising personnel policies for board approval, reviewing job descriptions, establishing a salary structure, and annually reviewing staff salaries. It may also be in involved with reviewing benefit packages.

Compensation

This variant of the personnel committee focuses on how much the nonprofit should pay the CEO. In some cases it also determines the ranges of compensation for the executive staff and the board authorizes the CEO to handle setting actual compensation for the executive staff and the rest of the staff.

A committee may be involved in the hiring of the ranking professional staff member whose job corresponds to his or her area of activity. In other words, if a university is hiring a new professional director of development, it is certain that members of the board-level development committee, with whom the development director will be closely working, will interview the top candidates for the job.

While the committees discussed above are typical, I also want to mention an approach for streamlined standing committees. Committees can proliferate and overwhelm boards and managers. To keep the committee structure very simple, some smaller organizations group activities into more broadly based committees, such as internal affairs, external affairs, and governance committees as suggested by David LaPiana in his well-known article, "Boards Should Only Have Three Committees" that appeared on BlueAvocado.org in June 2009.

Many boards are evolving and are works in progress. They're very dependent on the chair's personality, skill, and time invested and the professional staff. Committee work is substantive and is an opportunity to add your talents, skills, and own stamp on the organization. Committees are where you can get to know others in the nonprofit better and develop your own leadership. I have seen many future presidents start off as committee members. Before I get ahead of myself, next let's look at what to expect at board meetings. O

6

....

Board Meetings

*I can do things you cannot, you can do things I cannot; together
we can do great things.*

~ MOTHER TERESA

At your first board meeting of the Sunrise Charitable Foundation, you
should arrive a few minutes early so that you can become acclimated
and get better acquainted with your fellow board members. When you
enter the boardroom (whether dedicated or makeshift), you may find
displayed on a table by the door a nametag or table tent for each board
member and a stack of papers that you'll need during the meeting—the
meeting agenda, perhaps a copy of the previous meeting's notes prepared
by the secretary, and financial and other reports. You may also find
materials relating to an upcoming event that you're expected to attend,
such as the annual gala or fundraising auction.

These business-related materials should have been sent or e-mailed
to you well in advance of the meeting. You will have taken the time to
review them so that you are now fully briefed. (Do not wait to read them
at the meeting.) A well-run board spends time on issues of importance
that require thought and discussion not just reading updates and reports.
But people are fallible, and many board members forget to bring these
necessary documents (never you, of course!). It's the wise chair or

executive director who makes copies of these papers available at the meeting.

A side note here about organizing all the paper that comes with board service: I mentioned earlier that I recommend that board members be given "board books" or binders that consist of key organizational documents and training materials and which provide ample space for agendas and meeting notes. These board books are a great help, especially if all the materials handed out at board meetings come three-hole punched. If you don't get an organized binder or folder from the nonprofit, I suggest making one for yourself.

With the necessary materials, you are ready for the meeting. You should be given a nametag or table tent. It's difficult for anyone to remember the names of sixteen or twenty people whom they've just met, and the last thing you want to do is sit there at the meeting and feel like a fifth wheel because you don't know everyone's name. So stick that nametag on your jacket or blazer or place your table tent in front of your seat, and take comfort in the fact that there are other people who are also new or challenged at remembering names.

If you've been on the board for a while, you may use this time before the meeting to have a quick get-together with your committee so that you can review the report that the committee head will deliver.

At the appointed hour, the chair will take his or her place at the table, and everyone will follow suit. The savvy chair will have a small clock or wristwatch nearby on the table. Once you've become a board veteran, you will appreciate a board chair who keeps a sharp eye on the clock and ensures that every meeting is completed on time.

The chair will call the meeting to order. At the first meeting of the year, it is customary for the first order of business to be introductions of members and for the chair to give members the opportunity to say a few words about themselves. If for some reason the board chair does not do this, don't be shy: immediately stick your hand in the air, wait to be recognized by the chair, and suggest that it be done. The chair may be a bit flustered by your forwardness, but every other member will be very grateful.

Once introductions have been made, you're off and running! The basic meeting format has been described in the previous chapter; with luck the chair will guide the group through the agenda, and at the end of the meeting you'll feel as though your time has been well spent.

The treasurer's report is very important. When this report is given, you absolutely must have in front of you copies of the annual budget (usually a spreadsheet, but it might be columns on a Word document) and the year-to-date report. A key responsibility of the board is to compare the projected budget against the actual year-to-date figures. If a discrepancy (usually a shortfall) is seen, then the treasurer and finance committee (or, in a small organization, the entire board) need to determine the likely cause and propose a remedy. Reasons for a revenue shortfall can include economic conditions, poor planning, changing consumer tastes, an exhibit or program that flopped, or poor results from a fundraising effort. Reasons for expense increases can include rising energy prices, new regulations, vendor price increases, unfavorable judgments, insurance hikes, and unexpected maintenance or repair costs. It's up to you as a board member to be fully informed as to the financial condition of the organization, to weigh the significance of any discrepancies in actual versus projected figures, and to participate in the discussion about what, if any, actions need to be taken to get back on track.

MEMBER PARTICIPATION

Whether it is an extension of your professional work or a separate call of purpose and service, serving on the board can give you the opportunity to express your thoughts in meetings and to learn the accepted ways to conduct meetings and resolve conflicts should you become the chair. Working together with others on the board toward a common good nurtures a unique bond and sense of belonging, and by participating you will develop a stronger sense of ownership when you get involved in issues that make a difference to your community.

The responsibilities are both real and rewarding; you and your fellow board members are charged with acting as a group to advance the organization. This means that you'll need to be both attentive and participatory. Your insights and ideas are valuable, and you should not be reluctant to offer them in a spirit of mutual cooperation.

Be wary of board chairs or executive committees who seem to pre-decide every issue and want the board to rubber-stamp their decisions. This is not proper governance and makes your service pointless. This is the kind of behavior that you can get a feeling for by talking to current board members *before* you make your choice to join. After you join you will find out quickly enough if this is the case; if it is, it's up to you to decide for yourself whether you want to politely but persistently ask for more discussion about important topics or just do the best you can and then get off at the end of the year.

Board service can—and should—be meaningful. I hope it is for you. Experiencing good, productive board meetings is a big part of what makes board service rewarding. You are with people whom you respect, and you leave each meeting with a feeling of accomplishment.

And then there is the occasional high-maintenance colleague...

THE HIGH-MAINTENANCE BOARD MEMBER

It's rare that a board is composed entirely of people who are all dedicated, selfless, and sensitive to the process. The odds are good that in your board service you'll encounter a person who is a pain in the, um... *neck*. Such people can be well meaning but misguided. Here is a tongue-in-cheek (but serious) survey of some of these types and what they do that can aggravate their colleagues. You've probably met these types at work or in your community. They are generally harmless, but you—and your board chair—will have a happier time if you're prepared in advance to handle them. The key is to modify their behavior in a way that's tactful and doesn't make them lose face.

Those extreme cases, where enough members of the board want to get rid of someone who's disruptive, I'll discuss in a later chapter.

Dina Derailer

Imagine this: You're at the board meeting and everyone is discussing the upcoming fundraising gala. It's a charity auction with dinner, held at a local function hall. This is what the organization has presented every year for the past decade, and each year the event makes lots of money. Everyone loves it. The event is two weeks away.

Suddenly Dina Derailer raises her hand. The chair duly recognizes her. Dina says, "I heard last week that the function hall is going out of business. They're bankrupt!"

What? This is horrifying news! The chair questions Dina. How did you hear this? From whom? The chair then asks the person who is heading up the events committee: Have you heard this? Is it true? Are we in big trouble? Do we have to find another venue?

Panic sets in. The events person asks to be excused to call the facility. The board meeting has run off the rails.

If Dina knew this before, why did she wait until the meeting to share the news? Successful board meetings are about order. Items to be discussed must appear on the agenda; the chair, along with the relevant committees, should anticipate the course of every discussion. Issues to be discussed must always be vetted in advance. Board members need to arrive at the meeting ready to offer plausible solutions. And if there is bad news, it should not be sprung on the board at the meeting. It is better quietly discussed well before the meeting. In this case, Dina should have informed the committee chair or staff person as soon as she heard the news.

Of course, it's terrific if someone has a brilliant idea on the spur of the moment; that's a good thing! But it should be offered as part of a discussion where new ideas are being solicited.

The Blowhard

The board is discussing a new initiative, such as an education program to be held on weekends. There are costs involved, and it is uncertain whether funding can be found to make the program work. There is a lot of lively participation, and some great ideas are offered as the meeting progresses.

Suddenly Bob Blowhard starts talking about a dude ranch that he visited on his recent trip to Colorado and how the weekends were really busy on the dude ranch because the world-class resident chef always prepared special gourmet dinners on Saturday nights that were served in the dude ranch's spectacular glass-enclosed atrium that had a view of the Rocky Mountains. The steak was unbelievable. "It's true what they say about grass-fed beef being so much better than..." As Bob drones on about this fantastically irrelevant topic, board members fidget in their seats and shoot glances at the chair that say, *Please make this person stop!*

The same type of person who dominates a conversation at work will show up on a board, too. It's just a fact of life. This is where you need a firm but tactful board chair who, during one of those inevitable microseconds when Bob must pause to take a breath, can quickly say, "That's fascinating, Bob. Thank you. Does anyone else have a comment to make about the weekend education program proposal?"

The rule is this: *Stick to the business at hand.* A board meeting is not the place for individual members to regale others about irrelevant topics.

The Micro-Discusser

A common problem at board meetings arises during committee reports. Let's say that the Buildings Committee head, Mindy Micro-Discusser, is giving her report about the plans to repaint the reception area. The committee is considering paint colors and the type of paint to be used. Suddenly Mindy and her committee co-head, Mark Micro-Discusser, begin talking to each other. The topic is whether California paints, which the contractor wants to use, are in fact better than Sherwin-

Williams, which Mark recently used on his house. As Mark and Mindy engage in a spirited discussion as to the various attributes of different brands of paint, the other fourteen members of the board sit and twiddle their thumbs. The minutes tick by as the chair allows this inane discussion to drag on. Finally the chair says, "Okay, Mark and Mindy, thanks very much. Please get back to us at the next meeting with your recommendation. Is there anything else?"

This leads to another rule of successful board meetings: *Committee business should be done outside the meeting.* The whole point of having committees is that they can focus on specific issues that the board should not have to deal with as a group. Instead of discussing the issue at the board meeting, Mark and Mindy should have simply reported to the board, "After performing diligent research, we recommend that the organization use California paints for the reception area. You will see the cost in your budget."

Let's say that one member of the board, Julie, thinks this is a mistake. She can say, "Mindy, do you mind if I talk to you after the meeting about this? I have some thoughts about paint."

Then the chair can say, "Thank you, Mark and Mindy for your report. You can talk with Julie after the meeting. Let's move on."

This is not to say that substantive issues should not be discussed with the full board. If Mindy had said, "We want to tear down the existing reception area and build a new one," this would obviously require the full board's attention.

The Rock

This type is not overtly harmful, but you wonder why they're on the board. Richard Rock will sit there hour after hour, month after month, and say nothing. When the chair asks for committee volunteers, Richard never holds up his hand. He just sits there.

An adroit chair will notice this and try to politely draw him out by saying, "Any comments? Richard, what do you think about the proposal to tear down the reception area?" The chair can also contact Richard outside of a meeting and talk to him about his participation and suggest a possible committee assignment that would appeal to him.

The Mouse and Negative Chairs

It's easy enough to imagine the unpleasantness of an imperial chair that treats the board members as his or her personal servants. The opposite type can be equally difficult. Martha Mouse somehow got herself made chair—perhaps she was too non-confrontational to refuse the offer! Unfortunately, she lacks the confidence to manage the group. Martha Mouse calls the meeting to order and then lets the meeting meander along without firm guidance. People like Bob Blowhard and Mindy Micro-Discusser dominate the discussions, which makes everyone else irritated and feeling as though their time were being wasted. Meetings run overtime and nothing gets decided because board members hold conflicting views that Martha can't—or won't—force the board to choose between.

A close cousin of Martha Mouse is Nathan Negative. This chair is adverse to any bold proposal or initiative that carries risk.

A capital campaign to build a new dormitory? *No, no.... Not now. The timing isn't right.*

Would so-and-so give us a donation? *No, no.... He won't.*

Can we stay open late on Thursday nights? *No, no.... It would be too expensive.*

The only thing that Nathan likes is the status quo. Unfortunately, remaining static is not a good long-term strategy!

Depending upon the personal dynamics of the board, there may not be much that you, a regular board member, can do about a timid or naysayer chair. If confident enough, the executive director or CEO of the organization can sit next to the hesitant chair at meetings and gently nudge him or her along. You may also want to propose a training session for the entire board (no names mentioned!) with a focus on leadership.

This is something that the executive director or relevant board committee may be able to facilitate.

Don't forget! A nonprofit is only as effective as its board.

YOUR ROLE AT THE MEETING

Since you are *not* one of the above bothersome types, you are well positioned to be an effective board member and to derive real satisfaction from your board service. Here are some tips that will make your service more rewarding and will help you make a contribution during meetings.

Understand the key governance questions that are being presented.

Before the meeting, review the materials that you should have been sent, including the upcoming agenda and financials. If you are not sure about something, call the board chair or the relevant committee head. If there is a major project on the horizon and you're not equipped to contribute, you may want to request training. This is very common with long-term initiatives, such as capital and endowment campaigns. Many board members don't know how they're structured, and training is vital to get the board positioned well.

Contribute your expertise.

You were asked to be on the board for a reason—you have something to bring to the table. Don't hold back! Share your knowledge and give your opinions during discussion. If a call is made for new members of a committee that is in your area of interest, go for it. You may be the type of person who doesn't enjoy speaking up in front of groups— in this case, the assembled board—and by serving on a committee, you can make a strong contribution behind the scenes.

Don't be rushed into decision making if more information is required.

Sometimes people with forceful personalities will try to steamroll a decision through the board. They may even—through subtle means or overtly—try to make you feel as though you're anti-progress or not in touch. Resist such pressure. You owe it to yourself, the organization, and (most of all) to the people served by the organization to make the best decision you can, which means being well informed.

Ask how a particular action fits with the organization's mission and into the strategic plan.

Keep the big picture in focus. Call out *mission creep,* which refers to a project that may on the surface seem very appealing but which may bend the organization away from its primary focus and responsibilities.

Leave the meeting armed with information.

At end of the meeting, understand exactly what is needed from you and what future dates you need to mark on your calendar. After the meeting, do any necessary follow-ups. You should receive the minutes of the meeting within a few days and definitely well before the next meeting.

Having reviewed what makes for a pleasant and productive meeting, let's take a look at where much of the heavy lifting takes place: on the board committees. O

7

··

Committee Work

Individual commitment to a group effort—that is what makes a team work, a company work, a society work, a civilization work.

~ **VINCE LOMBARDI**

As you grow accustomed to being a member of the board of the Sunshine Charitable Foundation, you'll learn that committees largely do the day-to-day work of the board. The committee structure is an efficient way to tackle and dive into the work of the organization, expedite work by removing routine tasks from board consideration, utilize the specific talents and knowledge of the board, and permit broader participation by all board members. Many organizations require board members to participate in at least one committee.

What's a *committee*? At its simplest level, a committee is an agile group of people who are focused on one project or operational area. Generally, board members form the core of any committee; they act as extensions of the board and report to the board. Their efforts may be augmented by members of the professional staff; outside experts or vendors; and additional "civilian" volunteers, who are neither paid staff nor board members.

For example, the special events committee in charge of planning the annual fundraising gala may be assisted by the organization's director of development, his or her assistants, and several—even dozens of—regular volunteers who donate their time and expertise to the organization.

The finance committee will likely work in close harmony with the organization's finance manager and the outside accountants, investment advisors, tax specialists, and auditors.

In Chapter 5, I provided an overview of the most common board-level committees. As a board member, it will be your job—a happy one, hopefully—to find a place for yourself on the committee that's most closely aligned with your personal interests and skills. If you are an accountant, the finance committee would be a natural fit. If you enjoy planning events, you might feel comfortable on the special events committee.

As far as the day-to-day operations of committees go, effective teamwork and communication are key. And while it's possible that you may find yourself on a committee with one of the bothersome types described previously, I think that people who volunteer for committee work tend to be focused and have realistic expectations. But, as everywhere in life, if you're stuck with a bothersome type, you sometimes just have to smile and do the best you can.

The Committee's Charge

If you are considering joining a committee, the very first question you should ask is "What's our charge or goal?"

The goal must have these qualities:

1. It must be measurable.

2. It must have a deadline.

3. It must involve either some sort of certification or a deliverable.

A certification might be a study that concludes that the organization is in compliance with certain regulations and that no action is needed.

More commonly, the goal of the committee is a defined deliverable. It can take many forms:

- A feasibility study for a capital campaign

- An amount of money raised by a special event

- The annual audit

·• Hiring a new CEO or executive director

- Identifying and inviting new board members

- Replacing old infrastructure, such as the inefficient boiler in the basement

- Writing a grant for a project

Some standing committees, such as the budget committee, do more or less the same thing every year. Other ad hoc committees are formed for a special task that may not be repeated, such as buying a new boiler for the basement.

MEMBERS

To get the work done, committees need members—people like you. Some committees may consist of only two board members, who are, therefore, co-chairs of the committee. Other committees have a chair (who is either appointed by the board chair or chosen by the committee members) and lots of members. Typically, special events committees tend to be very large because planning a fundraising event involves hundreds of tasks related to the venue, catering, entertainment, invitations, the program, or perhaps an auction; and each of these tasks may have its own subcommittee.

Every board committee will have a staff member assigned to it. In small organizations this may be the executive director. It may also be the development director, human resources specialist, finance manager, program director, visitor services manager, or membership manager—whoever handles the activity pursued by the committee.

The committee may include regular volunteers who are not board members. The committee may also work with an outside consultant or expert. For example, a capital campaign committee that is charged with raising funds for a new building may include these people:

- Two or more board members, one of whom is the committee chair

- The organization's director of development

- One or more volunteers who are members of, or who support, the organization but aren't currently on the board (possibly past board members who are still active and are interested in this project)

- A paid capital campaign consultant

- Perhaps one or two big donors whom the organization wants to include in the planning process

- Possibly an architect, site planner, or building feasibility expert

MEETINGS

Depending upon the task and the members' availability, committees meet at various times and intervals. When you are considering joining a committee, one of the very first things you need to determine is whether or not you have the time to devote to the necessary meetings and if you and your committee colleagues can set a workable schedule.

If you find yourself the chair or co-chair, you will set the meetings for the committee. When my son was born, I left my job as a corporate attorney and became a full-time mom. For five years, I was a stay-at-home mom and a professional volunteer. I was involved in committees at my son's preschool, at our synagogue, and in our town. When my son started preschool and the kids were talking about their parents' professions, my son told his class that his mother's job was "going to meetings and talking on the phone."

That was pretty accurate.

Whether due to the sheer number of hours spent at and running meetings or to some innate ability, I became a meeting maven.

Based on my own experience, the following are some fundamental rules for running meetings with committee colleagues and volunteers.

Give Ample Notice with End Times

Set the date and time for each meeting as far in advance as possible. Generally, at the end of one meeting, you will decide the time and date of the next meeting. Tell your participants what time the meeting will end, and make sure it is not more than ninety minutes after your starting time. Peoples' time is valuable and scheduling can be difficult. Make sure your colleagues and volunteers know that you value and respect their time. After ninety minutes, people lose focus and productivity wanes.

Set an Inclusive Agenda

Set an agenda and send it in advance to allow for contributions from participants. Agendas must be adhered to with a little wiggle room for some deviations and flexibility as needed.

Give Clear Charges

Make sure everyone leaves the meeting understanding the next steps, clearly delineated tasks, and deadlines. *No one should leave without a task; if there are no tasks, the very existence of the committee is probably pointless.*

Keep Everyone in the Loop

Send your meeting minutes out within forty-eight hours after your meeting to inform people who could not attend and to allow for comments from those in attendance while they still remember the meeting. This also ensures that you compose the meeting minutes while the meeting and the outcomes are fresh in your mind.

Say "Thank You!"

This is one of the most underutilized phrases in the nonprofit world, but one of the most important. Say it after every interaction with a volunteer. You can't say it enough!

People who lead meetings in the nonprofit world should consider themselves project managers and think about how each meeting moves their project or projects closer to completion. They must remember that—unlike in for-profit settings—people are not being paid to participate. Therefore, nonprofits have to be even more careful to ensure efficient, effective, and thoughtful meetings and always appreciate the volunteers and their time.

Expectations and Responsibilities

When serving on a board (as with any position, paid or volunteer), you will be happiest when you have a clear understanding of what is expected both of the committee and of you individually. You must have clarity in these areas:

• The charge and objectives of the committee

• The steps the committee needs to take to move its mission forward

• The timetable for completion of the steps

- The meeting schedule and the breakdown of the individual tasks to be accomplished (For large committees, such as special events, these can be delineated on a spreadsheet or by using a mind mapping or project management software or app.)

For a sample Committee Action Worksheet, please go to my website www.fridmanstrategies.com and use the password: **ONBOARD** to access the private download area.

If there is an expense budget, make sure it is realistic. If you are fundraising, make sure the goal is attainable and know where the funds are going. Many organizations try to avoid placing revenues from fundraising events into the general operating coffers because the board volunteers do not want the pressure of raising money for day-to-day expenses. Revenues from special events are often earmarked for things like scholarships, so that if the event falls short, the volunteers do not feel as though they are responsible for the organization being forced to cut back services or lay off staff.

As a committee chair or member, you may be required to sign a contract on behalf of the organization (for example, to hire the caterer for the dinner gala or a speaker at commencement). Simply use your best judgment; if a committee has a budget and the authority (actual, not merely implied) to commit and use the budget for its programs because the board delegated that to the committee, then the contract is valid. However, do not sign a contract and commit the organization unless you have been expressly authorized by the board to do so. Some organizations have rules specifying that any contract for over a certain amount must be signed by the CEO, CFO, president, or treasurer. Be sure to educate yourself on the policies and procedures for expenditures.

Serving on a committee can be deeply gratifying because you can use your skills and see the results of your work (for example, endowment money raised, the new wing built, and that audit completed).

In the next chapter, we will take a deeper look at the team that is responsible for the day-to-day operations at the nonprofit and at a relationship that can be key to an organization's forward movement in all areas—that of the board and the executive director. ○

8

....

The Executive Director, Staff, and Volunteers

Talent wins games, but teamwork and intelligence wins championships.

~ MICHAEL JORDAN

Hiring a New Executive Director

During your time as a board member at the Sunrise Charitable Foundation, the board may need to hire a new executive director (sometimes called CEO). If your organization is in search of new professional leadership, this is often the most important—and occasionally stressful—decision a board will make in many years and one you will want to take seriously.

The need to hire a new executive comes about either in a planned way as in the case of retirement or strategic restructuring, or it can be sudden due to personal circumstances or malfeasance. If a vacancy is created before a proper search can be conducted, the board will need to make interim arrangements for the organization's management. An acting leader is often put in place. The board should *never* rush to find a permanent replacement. Rather, it should make plans to continue the management of the organization while a search process is conducted.

Below are the steps and key questions involved in a typical process that a nonprofit undertakes for hiring a new leader.

1. Determining the Hiring Strategy

a. Putting together a search committee: An ad hoc hiring or search committee will be appointed by the board president and often comprises board members and other stakeholders who have an understanding of the executive position's requirement, such as community leaders, long-term donors, or volunteers. The search committee is responsible for formulating the executive director's job description and selecting the criteria against which to rate candidates for the position. The group usually includes an odd number of members in case the members cannot reach consensus and need to resort to voting. The committee will agree on a hiring strategy and process: whether or not to use an outside search firm, necessary tasks, schedules, and when and how to involve the staff and other board members.

b. Deciding to hire an outside recruiter or search consultant: While the board must own the hiring process, board members often do not have the particular skills required for finding top nonprofit talent. Frequently a board committee will work with a recruiter or an executive search firm specializing in nonprofit searches. The names of potential recruiters or search firms are often found by asking colleagues and board members for recommendations (at this nonprofit or others). One person from the committee will interview firms and understand their fees and services before bringing the summary of the choices to the search committee for selection. Once engaged, the firm and the search committee decide upon the geographic scope of the search, a timetable, and a preliminary salary range. The recruiter may offer salary comparables to aid the discussion.

2. Honing in on the Best Candidate for Your Organization

a. Determining the ideal candidate and writing a job description: The next step for a search committee is to determine the profile of the ideal candidate based on the organization's current and future needs. What are the knowledge, skills, abilities, and other characteristics needed in this position? What is the salary range that the organization can afford? What are the unique circumstances that the new leadership will face? Is there a capital or endowment campaign in the works that requires a skilled fundraising executive with similar experience? Are there merger talks on the horizon? Is the organization in trouble or looking to grow? For example, one of my clients was conducting a search during a financially troubling time in the organization's history. They were only interested in candidates with turn-around experience. Another client was in growth mode when they were looking for a new leader and were seeking someone who had scaled organizations before. A written job description is developed and usually approved by the full board before being finalized.

b. Advertising the position: The hiring committee advertises the vacancy in appropriate venues, targeting nonprofit job boards and websites and, occasionally, print publications specific to the industry or work of the organization. The committee will also post the job description on the organization's website and share it on social media as well as send it to the organization's mailing list and their own personal networks.

If you are using an outside firm, the recruiter will assist with or handle advertising the position and seeking qualified applicants. Good recruiters use face-to-face meetings and phone calls to their networks and respected nonprofit peers to seek out potential candidates. The best candidates are often those not looking to change employment.

3. Evaluating Candidates

a. Initial screening: If the search committee is not using an outside recruiter, the committee members will usually select one person to receive all applications and conduct a preliminary review to determine if an applicant appears to meet the stated criteria based on their e-mail, cover letter, resume, etc. You will be surprised how many people apply for jobs for which they are clearly not qualified! Applications that pass the initial round are then read through and further evaluated against the core criteria for the position. One or more members of the search committee (or even the entire committee) can do this.

b. The screening interviews: Ultimately, five to ten of the most suitable applications are chosen for a brief screening interview, usually conducted by telephone or Skype. From this group, a short list of three to five candidates is created for the in-person interviews. If the board is using an outside recruiter, the recruiter will conduct a similar process for applications they receive. Recruiters typically involve the search committee once they have a short list of candidates. Sometimes members of the search committee will participate in select screening interviews.

c. Checking references: Candidates can easily submit resumes that look impressive and they may even interview well. It is up to the search committee or the recruiter to uncover a candidate's actual productivity by speaking to his or her past work associates who have solid knowledge of their work record.

You'll find an excellent sample list of questions to ask when performing an Executive Reference Check in the private access area of our site; simply go to www.fridmanstrategies.com and use the password: **ONBOARD**.

d. Conducting final interviews: The committee interviews the final candidates. These interviews often take place outside business hours for the convenience of the volunteer board members who may have full-time jobs elsewhere. The candidate will also meet with the entire board for a formal and/or informal assessment.

e. Involving key staff and other stakeholders: Key staff members are kept informed of the process as it unfolds and, if possible, participate in the process. It is important to give them the opportunity to meet with the final candidates. Staff will have valuable insight. They will also appreciate being part of the process.

Other key stakeholders should be consulted as well. In the case of a school, parents may be invited to listen to the finalists speak and offer their feedback. In addition, important donors and community partners are also often asked to meet with candidates.

f. Debriefing and assessing: Once all the finalists are interviewed and the key constituencies have met with them, evaluations, impressions, and thoughts are collected usually either by survey or written notes.

The search committee is then charged with the task of assessing the finalists with all the information gathered throughout the process. The search committee must pick the best candidate while understanding that nobody is perfect. They must compare the apples and oranges of assets and liabilities that the various candidates have. Doing so is more of an art than a science!

4. The Hiring Process

a. Agreeing on a candidate: Once the search committee has settled on a candidate for recommendation, they inform the board. They ask the board (by vote) to authorize the search committee to extend an offer to the chosen candidate for the position at a designated salary for a specific period of time.

b. Making the offer: Once the board agrees on the best candidate, the search committee chair contacts the chosen applicant and makes a verbal offer, then follows with an official offer letter by e-mail or post.

c. Negotiating the details: If the candidate accepts the offer, the member of the search committee or an employment lawyer who is on the board or who volunteers time to the organization will then negotiate the terms of an agreement. Sometimes a recruiter may act as a good-faith broker, trusted by both the committee and the final candidate to negotiate the employment contract.

d. Entering into an employment agreement: Once the candidate and the negotiator agree on terms, an employment agreement is executed. The agreement sets out the specific conditions of employment including the agreed compensation, vacation, medical insurance, retirement benefits, and other parameters of employment, such as probation period and provision for termination. It also includes standard conditions such as confidentiality, and in some cases, goals or targets that the executive director must fulfill within a certain time frame.

5. Establishing a Good Relationship with the New Executive Director

After investing in the search process, the committee may work with the executive committee or the personnel committee of the board to make sure that new executive's tenure is off to a strong start.

a. Proper orientation: If the new leader will be moving to take this position, someone from Sunrise Charitable Foundation should introduce and welcome the new executive and his or her family to the area and help them get acclimated. It is also customary for the board to arrange for the new executive to have meet-and-greets with key stakeholders both internally and externally.

b. Setting clear expectations: Soon after the new executive director starts, the board chair and executive should meet to establish ground rules for communication and define clear expectations for each other.

c. Planning for formal evaluation: Depending on the terms of the employment agreement, there may be a ninety-day probationary period. If so, continued employment is dependent on a successful performance review assessment. Probationary periods protect employers from hires who are inefficient or poor fits for the organization. A formal evaluation is given after an initial six-months or one-year period. Board feedback is typically given to the executive director on his or her initial performance in a private meeting by the chair.

Through participating in the hiring of a new leader for the Sunrise Charitable Foundation, you have had the unique and important opportunity to influence the organization for a very long time.

Selecting the best executive director is important because of his or her key role as manager and professional leader of the organization. To carry out all of its work, the Sunrise Charitable Foundation utilizes the talents of many people in many positions. They can be roughly organized into four groups: the board, the executive director (ED), the paid staff (both senior and junior), and the volunteers who are not board members. In the course of your work on the board, you'll be interacting with members of the other three groups. Here are some insights into those positions and how you can ensure those interactions will be positive and productive.

THE EXECUTIVE DIRECTOR AND FOUR KEYS TO BEING A SUCCESSFUL ONE

During the Cuban Missile Crisis in 1961, *The New York Times* said that President Kennedy had the loneliest job in the world. A lot has changed since that time, not only in politics and the private sector but also in the nonprofit sector. In this day and age, the executive director of a nonprofit organization might, in fact, have one of the loneliest jobs in the world.

The executive director is expected to be the Wizard of Oz, a person who is a visionary CEO, an operating manager, a programmatic genius with passion, a leader both internally and externally, and a skilled fundraiser. Besides having so many hats to wear, the executive director is supposed to do everything with a magical turn of the hand and with limited resources.

Being everything to everybody, sometimes on a shoestring budget, is a tall order to fill. The position is lonely because there aren't very many other wizards at the top and very few others whom the executive director can let behind the curtain. In a small organization, being the executive director is an especially lonely job because there aren't very many people in the organization and even fewer at the top. The executive director does have a board, but the board consists of volunteers who are giving the organization a small percentage of their time and don't have the time (or desire) to also work through routine high-level thinking with the executive director. The relationship that the executive director has with the board is that of employee and boss, not of peers. This means that the executive director cannot over-ask and cannot over-share.

The executive director always needs to be the positive face of the organization. There are round tables, but these are rarely places where directors come together and spill all of their—or the organization's—challenges. Instead, the roundtables are fantastic resources for the directors to gain awareness in general as to what is happening in the nonprofit community outside of their organization and to spot trends.

As a board member, you are part of the team that is responsible for hiring, evaluating, and possibly replacing the executive director. As a board member, understanding the challenges of the executive director's job and offering to be a thought partner or sounding board to the executive director can be a bridge-building gesture and of enormous help to both sides.

As you approach your important board responsibilities, it's a good idea to keep in mind the critical distinctions between board and management. Both the organization's board and its management have to understand the distinctive role of the other and have a set of expectations that are in line with reality.

It's the board's job to set policy and long-term plans; approve or remove programs; select, oversee, and compensate the executive director; approve the operating budget recommended by management; raise funds; and oversee the endowment. Management generally is responsible for selection and supervision of staff, routine development efforts, recommendation and implementation of the budget, running of the programs and services, and establishment of operation procedures. The power of the board resides with the full board, not with individual board members. The board sets standards to measure how well management performs and intervenes when required to see that management carries out its duties.

A Successful Executive Director and the Board

In his or her relationship to the board, the executive director should help the board to both assemble and address the information that shapes the strategic direction of the organization. As a member of the board, you can expect an effective executive director to consistently follow these four action steps, which can help the board to govern effectively and be less concerned with micromanagement.

1. The executive director should help develop and implement the comprehensive strategic plan and supplement it with regular progress reports. Holding the strategic plan at the forefront will keep the board's sights focused on the long-term goals and mission of the organization and help it develop its own annual work plans. Regular reports that reflect performance indicators of the plan (revenue raised, constituents served, program outcomes) will both provide evidence for the evaluation of the executive director and keep board members aware of progress toward organizational goals.

2. Before every board meeting, the executive director needs to provide the board with relevant materials and reports along with an explanation as to why the materials need to be seen by the board. He or she must ensure that board members understand how specific agenda items relate to the organization's strategy and what kind of action or discussion is required by the board on each item.

3. To keep the board focused on the central issues, the executive director needs to facilitate board and board–committee discussions. He or she should strive to engage the board in a dialogue among themselves that leads to consensus building. When necessary, the executive director will

respectfully refer to organizational policies that define the limits of the board's decision-making power.

4. The executive director should personally thank individual board members for their service every time he or she interacts with them. While the executive director is technically the employee of the board, and as a group the board is the executive director's superior, board members tend see the executive director as someone who is getting paid to do what they are doing for free. Of course, it's not as simple as that, but the perception remains that the board member is the one to whom gratitude should be expressed at every opportunity.

Nonprofit magic happens when an organization has a strong professional leader and a dedicated and engaged board and when the two have a collaborative and well-tuned working relationship. Hopefully, this will be the case at Sunrise Charitable Foundation.

Unfortunately, sometimes there is either a take-charge management professional or a super-charged board driving an organization with its counterpart marginalized. In other cases, both the lay and professional leaders are strong, but the working relationship between the two is weak or worse, dysfunctional.

Organizations with a Dominant Professional

When organizations are dominantly professionally led and driven, one danger is that the volunteer board coasts and is not adequately engaged in its fiduciary responsibilities, neither in terms of approving and monitoring the budgets nor in fundraising; therefore, the potential capacity of the organization is not realized. In these cases, the board often also fails to fulfill its duty of setting the strategic course and direction of the organization unless being led or prodded to do so by the executive director.

Another side effect of a professionally driven organization is that the paid leader often chooses to withhold or delay information from the board, knowing that the board is unlikely to respond or be active. Often, this is information the board should have. The shouldering of the burden or the shielding the board by the professional can cause the board's nonfeasance. Moreover, when not being properly engaged and utilized, board members who are looking for meaningful service will seek other opportunities. Superstar board members don't want to be rubber stamps.

When the executive director does not believe that the board is a true working partner, the job becomes incredibly stressful and lonely. If lucky, the executive director can use senior staff as sounding boards or engage outside resources, such as a coach. When an organization is so staff driven, it is vulnerable when the professional leadership turns over.

Organizations with a Dominant Board

In the instances where the *board* is the primary driver of the organization, a common problem is micro-management of the executive director by the board. In some extreme cases, the professional is so micro-managed that he or she is diminished to a figurehead. If, as a result, the staff no longer has confidence in the executive director and loses respect for him or her, the executive director may lose control of the staff. When the board repeatedly and egregiously crosses the line, retention of the professional leader can be a problem.

Another danger is that volunteers who do the lion's share of work for an organization ultimately burn out or come to resent their roles. A corollary follows that other board members are reluctant or suspicious of taking leadership roles on overpowering boards; this occurs because of the example set that the volunteer board runs the show and, therefore, any board member must commit an inordinate amount of time to the organization. Most people don't want to compromise their paid careers or family time with overly-demanding volunteer responsibilities.

Strong Professional, Strong Board

If an organization is lucky enough to have both a strong professional and a strong board, the next step is working to ensure that their partnership is successful. Successful professional and volunteer relationships are based on four key components:

- Mutual respect and trust

- Shared vision

- Clear roles and responsibilities

- Clear, open, and continuous communication

Anytime any one of these components is lacking, the working relationship is weakened.

Making Magic between the Board and the Executive Director

Here's how an organization can work to attract and retain a stellar professional and a board leader both of whom are clear about their respective roles and who work well together to craft a vision and direction for the organization:

1. Hire or elect leaders who know how to work with other people and manage relationships. If leaders need help with managing their work relationships, invest in coaching.

2. Make sure that job descriptions both for board members and for professional staff are very clear, with distinct roles and responsibilities that include working with each other in a collaborative partnership.

3. Create a culture of openness, collaboration, and partnership for the organization by holding retreats, regularly inviting staff to board meetings, and establishing mentoring programs to promote dialogue and relationship building. Use outside facilitators for retreats and meetings to allow everyone in the organization to participate.

4. Have regular two-way reviews and establish annual goals that include benchmarks for working together and incentives for meeting the benchmarks.

5. Schedule regular (weekly or bi-weekly, if possible) meetings of the executive director and the board chair.

6. Share financial information regularly with the entire board regardless of how often your board meets.

7. Actively engage board members in development activities, especially joint executive director and board member solicitations.

8. Use strategic planning to engage both professional and volunteer leaders in the process and in measuring progress. Engage a professional strategic planner to make sure that all stakeholders are heard equally in the process.

9. Tend to both professional and volunteer succession planning to make sure that leaders can "come up the ranks" together.

10. Insist that everyone in the organization works in an honest, respectful, and transparent manner. Establish a zero-tolerance policy and enforce it.

The board–staff relationship is paradoxical. When acting in their governing role, the board must collectively exert authority and demand accountability from the executive director and his or her staff. But when acting in their supporting role, individual board members act to support and assist staff-led work.

It is hard to make magic, but when you do, you will find work is more fun and more meaningful for both the professional and the volunteer leaders, and the greatest potential of the organization is unleashed.

THE PROFESSIONAL STAFF AND VOLUNTEERS

At the Sunrise Charitable Foundation, there may be a staff of hundreds of people working in many departments, or there may be just a few employees working in the office with the executive director. Your contact with them may be formal and limited, or you may interact with one or more on a regular basis. If there's a senior staff—director of development, finance manager, curator of the museum—they may attend board meetings and serve on committees.

Your relationship with them is not the same as your relationship with the executive director. As a group, the board has the direct authority to oversee the executive director and his or her activities. In turn, it is part of the executive director's responsibilities to hire and oversee the professional staff. While the board may play a part in the hiring of senior staff—for example, by participating in job interviews—the board does not have direct operational oversight of the staff.

Therefore, your relationship to individual members of the staff is highly nuanced.

Let's say that you are a member of the special events committee and you are helping to plan the Sunrise Charitable Foundation annual gala. Serving with the board members and other volunteers on the gala committee is the director of development. Together with his or her staff, the director of development's role includes these functions:

- Providing administrative services, such as maintaining the prospect database, handling contract preparation, and coordinating meetings

- Making payments to vendors

- As needed, taking an active role in fundraising, such as selling ads in the gala program or soliciting sponsorships

- Advising the gala committee and liaising between the gala committee and other departments, such as marketing

It's a nuanced relationship because the director of development is not your employee, but he or she does have a professional obligation to both assist you and advise you. If this person is difficult to work with or is ineffectual, your only recourse is to complain to the person who provided this employee to you: the executive director.

Ideally, the gala committee—board members; non-board volunteers, such as a *friends-of* group; and staff—functions like a well-oiled machine, with no conflicts. That's what everyone wants, but sometimes people can feel pressured and worried about the success of the event. Tensions can build, and people can have expectations that cannot be fulfilled.

How you conduct yourself is important. It matters to the staff and to your fellow volunteers. Regardless of the challenges of the moment, you want to be the board member who is respected and whom the staff wants to please. You do not want to be the board member whom the staff complains about to the executive director.

At every nonprofit, the following scene has most likely happened— I guarantee you.

It's a perfectly lovely day, and work at the Sunrise Charitable Foundation is humming along nicely. Staff members are in their offices and work is getting done. Suddenly someone looks out the window to the parking lot.

"Ugh! Mrs. Crampton is here!" says the staff member. Sure enough, marching up to the front door is the board member whom no one wants to see. Word spreads quickly throughout the office.

"Whom does she want to talk to?" someone asks. "The development officer on the gala committee?"

Panic sets in as Mrs. Crampton approaches the front desk.

"I'm here to see Suzy!" she bellows to the receptionist.

"Suzy is on a call," replies the receptionist. "She'll be with you as soon as she can."

"I haven't got all day!" insists Mrs. Crampton. "Tell her to *get off the phone.* The flower arrangements on the tables are all wrong. Doesn't she know this?"

"The flower arrangements are wrong?" says the receptionist. "I'm very sorry to hear that."

"It's a *disaster!*" says Mrs. Crampton.

The executive director, having heard the commotion, bravely emerges from her office. With a smile on her face she approaches the unhappy board member.

"Why Mrs. Crampton, what an unexpected pleasure," she says in a friendly but respectful tone. "How may I help you?"

After a few minutes of soothing and flattering Mrs. Crampton, peace is restored, and the executive director, who has much better things to do with her time than placate a demanding board member, gets back to work.

Don't be a Mrs. Crampton! Be the board member whom everyone is happy to see because you are empathetic and understanding of the professional lives and challenges of the salaried employees.

A good relationship between the board and professional staff is grounded in honesty and respect, facilitated by communication. Empathy helps too. You'll develop this through seeing the work of the nonprofit through the eyes of the staff.

Senior Staff

Working under pressure, the senior staff is often overworked and underpaid relative to their for-profit counterparts. While they don't have all the resources of a for-profit company, they experience many of same demands. These positions tend to have lots of turnover, as similar jobs in the private sector often pay more.

Senior staff seek out sounding boards and mentors. They want to be appreciated, valued, and taken seriously. When they have to follow up with you to get you to do what you promised to do, it takes time away from their primary tasks.

Saying "thank you" to them goes a long way! And they, in turn, should be saying "thank you" to you. If it sounds as if people in the nonprofit sector should be constantly thanking each other, you're right. You cannot say "thank you" too often—to the staff, to the executive director, to your fellow volunteers.

If you are having a good experience with a staff member on a project, tell the person's boss! Every executive director wants to know how the staff is performing and whether or not you, the board volunteer (and probably a donor too), are happy. Conversely, if a staff member isn't getting the job done, privately inform the executive director. It is the executive director's job to oversee the staff, and you need to let him or her do it.

Junior Staff

Employees who are further down the organizational chart may have direct contact with you, or they may only see you passing in the hallway on the way to a meeting. Remember to be empathetic. They are working for lower wages, may have less experience, and may be nervous about their position in the organization. It is possible that they want to communicate with you but are reluctant or do not know how. You have to seek their input to the extent that it is appropriate.

Do not ask staff for favors (such as complimentary tickets to events) or to do jobs for you. It puts them in an uncomfortable position, and outside of a committee structure there is really no reason why you should be asking them to do anything for you.

Being friends with staff can be compromising; while it's good to share with board staff your feelings and thoughts, keep lines in place for confidential information. As a board member, recuse yourself from any issue particular to your staff friend if it comes before the board.

Resist the desire to micromanage staff members. Managing staff is the job of the executive director. Let him or her do the job and help them to the extent that you can. Remember, the nonprofit sector seldom has the same resources and staff as the private sector. Staff often feels overworked, undervalued, and undercompensated.

And always say "thank you."

Volunteers

Many organizations are supported by the efforts of volunteers who are not board members. These volunteers may belong to a feeder organization that grooms people for future board service; the organization may have a general name, such as "auxiliary," or a specific name, like "The Sunrise Council" or the "Friends of Sunrise." They may belong to a specialized group, such as a young-peoples' group, or perhaps they are involved only through their activities on one committee, such as the gala or golf tournament. Volunteers may be museum docents, hospital volunteers, or theatre ushers; they may be students looking to gain experience or retired persons who want to stay active.

Volunteers serving in any capacity are just like you; only they're not on the board. They're giving of their time with no material reward. Many nonprofit organizations could not remain solvent without the contributions of volunteers; and of course, as a board member you'll treat every volunteer with the same respect and kindness that you expect to receive from them.

A successful nonprofit is a team effort. As the foundation of the team, the board hires the executive director, who sets the tone for the organization's culture and hires and manages the staff. The staff, in turn, engages and works with the volunteers. As in any organization, personalities run the gamut. A good nonprofit leader always rallies around the mission and asks the entire team to stay focused on serving the population in need.

Next, we will turn to how the organization charts its course of action through strategic planning. ○

9

STRATEGIC PLANNING

Plans are nothing; planning is everything.

~DWIGHT D. EISENHOWER

In addition to friendraising and fundraising—whether for an annual fund, a capital campaign, an endowment campaign, a special event, or a grant—you should be asked during your term to monitor the implementation of the Sunrise Charitable Foundation's strategic plan and to participate in long-term planning.

A strategic plan is like a road map in that it provides direction as the organization works to carry out its mission and move toward fulfilling its vision. But it is not carved in stone, and it is not a static document that, once it has been approved, is shoved into a filing cabinet and forgotten. A functional strategic plan is a living document that provides guidance and may also be amended or revised as conditions change. It is meant to be used and evaluated on a rolling basis, not to sit on the shelf.

Strategic planning is a process designed to support leaders in being intentional about their goals and the methods to best pursue their vision. The process is strategic because it involves choosing how best to respond to a dynamic and sometimes challenging environment. It is about choosing directions, prioritizing, and setting objectives. Generally, strategic plans take a view of three to five years into the future. We rarely see plans that are longer, because in today's fast-moving culture conditions change rapidly.

In terms of process, usually an *ad hoc* strategic planning committee will be appointed to develop a draft strategic plan to present to the board for approval. In some cases the entire board serves as a *de facto* strategic planning committee.

The process seeks to assess where the organization is now, where it wants to go and how it will get there by laying out the road map and setting strategic objectives, goals, and actions.

During the strategic planning process, if the only input is from the board and key staff, an organization gets a very narrow view of itself. To have meaning and validity, the process must bring together the perspective of multiple stakeholders of the nonprofit. These stakeholders include the board, professional staff, volunteers, clients, funders, partners, government agencies, and even suppliers. They all have a role in supporting the potential success of the nonprofit, and they each have a unique and valuable perspective.

Soliciting the input of the multiple stakeholders involved with the nonprofit is important for the insights and also to create buy-in for whatever plan is designed. The strategic planning committee, often with the help of a consultant, will want to discuss several questions: What do we need to ask? From whom do we need to hear? How will we get that information? Who will be responsible for getting it? Often questionnaires, interviews, focus groups, or visioning sessions will be used. Since the data is collected and interpreted, both organizational issues and client impacts will be revealed for the nonprofit to begin strategic planning.

KEY COMPONENTS OF A STRATEGIC PLAN

Strategic planning is essentially a process of organization alignment. A strategic plan provides a nonprofit with an integrating mechanism and should include the following five aspects:

Determine the As-Is Baseline of the Organization

Before you can plan, it is important to have a factual assessment of the current status of the organization and the environment in which it operates. This includes the quantitative and qualitative data on those that apply: members, programs or services, budget and finance, fundraising, marketing and communication, leadership, facilities/building and grounds, operations and professional staff. A SWOT analysis is performed to look at the organization's internal Strengths and Weaknesses and the Opportunities and Threats of the external environment in which it operates—trends, demographics, competition, and the economy. The goal is to leverage strengths, take advantage of opportunities, compensate for weaknesses, and minimize threats.

Confirm or Define the Mission and Whom You Serve

As discussed in Chapter 2, the mission is the overarching expression of the purpose of the nonprofit. It describes in simple terms what the nonprofit currently does, whom it does it for, and what impacts it will have. The strategic plan confirms the current mission or may redefine it. The plan should clearly articulate the client or target audience, the needs of the client, and how the organization meets the defined needs of the client. Clearly defining the audience for the nonprofit's services or programs and the exact benefits (or outcomes) they desire provides the nonprofit with the focus for its strategic plan.

Establish or Confirm the Vision

The vision speaks to the ultimate impact that the organization wants to have on the community and the kind of world that it wants to see in the future.

Establish Priorities and Long-Term Objectives

These long-term strategic focus areas span a timeline horizon of usually no more than five years. They answer the question of what the nonprofit must focus on to achieve its vision.

Integrate Long-Term Strategic Objectives with Short-Term Goals, Priorities and Actions

Goals and priorities transform the strategic objectives into specific performance targets. Goals and priorities should be defined for the five basic functional areas for all nonprofits: programs and services, funding, marketing and communications, operations, and buildings and infrastructure. The actual assignments for board and staff to address are expressed as a one-year action plan that details how the goals will be accomplished. The action plan states *what* will be done, by *when,* and by *whom*; it also includes the measures of success. This becomes the agenda for the board for the coming year and provides the proper balance between planning and acting to assure movement against the strategic plan. The nonprofit still has to meet its day-to-day responsibilities, so the key is to make this challenging but not overwhelming.

Sometimes the strategic planning process requires a re-boot of the mission and even of the name of the organization. Here's an example.

THE LARZ ANDERSON AUTO MUSEUM

The Larz Anderson Auto Museum's story is a great example of reviewing and updating the mission to support the strategic direction of an organization. In 1949, a wealthy widow named Isabel Anderson passed away. She left a portion of her vast estate to the city of Brookline, Massachusetts, where she and her late husband Larz Anderson had maintained a mansion and an enormous carriage house. In the carriage house was stored their irreplaceable collection of antique automobiles—steam cars, electric cars, limousines, roadsters—all from the early twentieth century, and all in original condition.

A group of auto enthusiasts quickly formed a 501(c)(3) nonprofit museum with the goal of preserving and displaying the priceless car collection in the carriage house. The organization was eventually named The Museum of Transportation.

Fast-forward fifty years. At the turn of the new century the museum was struggling, the cars were in poor condition, and the board was unable to focus on priorities. Creating a strategic plan was impossible because of the internal conflicts between the original stated mission of the museum and the museum's reality. There was a real danger that the museum would become insolvent.

A new executive director and new board president realized that the museum must rebuild its foundation.

The first step was to rewrite the mission statement, and they soon came to the conclusion that the museum would need a new name as well. The process began with a series of open meetings that anyone could attend. These community meetings, which were presided over by the board president, often became contentious; for example, one faction consisting of "car guys" was reluctant to restore the focus of the museum on the old Anderson car collection, preferring to highlight modern vehicles.

Although this wasn't the case at this museum, such brainstorming sessions—indeed, often the entire process—can be well managed by an external, impartial consultant. Outside consultants, such as I, have the training to guide the organization through the process, and they provide an atmosphere of objectivity that can be reassuring to staff and other stakeholders, who may be inclined to believe that the proposed changes are being forced upon them by an autocratic board president or planning committee.

As for the name of the museum, just about everyone agreed that since the museum neither collected nor displayed things like boats and airplanes, the name "Museum of Transportation" was absurd. The operational focus had always been on cars. The challenge was to agree on a new name, which had to be in alignment with the new mission. After several months of lively discussion and soul-searching, the new mission statement and name were approved by unanimous vote of the board:

"The Larz Anderson Auto Museum is a 501(c)(3) nonprofit educational and cultural institution dedicated to the preservation of our varied collections including the world renowned Anderson Car Collection, and to the education of the public on the automobile and its impact upon society through changing exhibits. In addition and central to the Museum's mission is the preservation of the enduring legacy of Larz and Isabel Anderson."

Thus the name and the mission were both brought into tighter focus. Any and all initiatives, including exhibits, could now be rationally planned against a set of standards that was much better defined than the word "transportation," which, given the organization's size and capabilities, was hopelessly broad. Strategic planning could now move ahead on a secure foundation. In addition, the mission statement included a reference to Larz and Isabel Anderson, who had originally formed the collection (beginning in 1899, they had bought a new "horseless carriage" every year, and had carefully maintained their growing fleet) and in whose carriage house the museum operated.

Today, the museum is stable and successful, and visitors have a much better idea of what they can expect when they walk through the doors.

Take off the Rose-Colored Glasses

In order for strategic planning to be worthwhile, it has to establish an accurate and realistic as-is baseline of where the organization is at, the external environment in which it operates, and its capacity to implement plans. To effectuate change, boards and management have to be able to take off their rose-colored glasses and admit to themselves the truths that they often don't want to say out loud. Here are a few examples:

- "Our mission has drifted or is no longer relevant."

- "We are too dependent on a few donors or sources of financial support."

- "Our numbers are artificial."

- "We are losing market share and can't seem to regain momentum."

- "We are not attracting strong leadership or are not developing our leaders."

- "Our brand is irreparably damaged."

- "We don't have the right professionals in place."

Not being able to see the truth—or perhaps more appropriately stated, not wanting to state the obvious—gets in the way of organizations being able to make the necessary changes and to overcome the challenges they face and to innovate.

Strategic planning processes are not the time for puffing, job protecting, sugarcoating, or self-congratulating. If boards aren't able to have honest conversations and identify and face their challenges head on, the organizations are wasting valuable time that could be spent addressing the real issues that stand in the way of operating in a healthy, efficient, effective, and sustainable way.

If the board is open to honest and self-critical assessments, the organization will be stronger for it and will be able to make tough decisions and embrace the changes necessary to survive in a competitive environment. The key is to reward the truth and don't shoot the messengers.

If you want to have a resilient, sustainable, growth-orientated organization, the boardroom must be a sanctuary of truth—especially when it comes to strategic planning. Ask questions. Don't be afraid to insist that board members and staff tell it like it is.

No book about board service would be complete without a discussion of the saga of the Barnes Foundation. While there are more than a few museums whose activities are partly or wholly defined by the will of the deceased founder or original benefactor—the Isabella Stewart Gardner Museum in Boston is a good example—perhaps none have faced challenges as daunting as the Barnes Foundation. It is a classic case of how strategic planning can be hampered—or even made impossible—by conditions that ensure that any rational long-range plan must be rejected because of pre-existing conditions.

THE BARNES FOUNDATION

It's the job of the board, working with the organization's stakeholders, to formulate the forward-looking strategic plan. While this process is never routine, sometimes the board and CEO come to the inescapable conclusion that in order to survive, the organization needs to make significant changes, such as a new building or a change in location. The story of the Barnes Foundation shows how the strategic planning process can be derailed when two sides see reality differently.

An American educational art and horticultural institution, the Barnes Foundation was founded in 1922 by Albert C. Barnes, a chemist who collected art after making a fortune in the pharmaceuticals industry. It was located in Merion, Pennsylvania, a suburb of Philadelphia.

In that year, Barnes chartered the Barnes Foundation as an educational institution. He selected a location in the unincorporated township of Merion, in Montgomery County, and commissioned architect Paul Cret to design a building complex. Barnes's conception was that his foundation would be as much a school as a public museum and that the art would serve to enlighten the foundation's students.

In an indenture of trust to be honored in perpetuity after his death, Barnes created detailed terms of operation. Public admission was limited to two days a week so that the school could use the art collection primarily for student study. The trust also prohibited the loan of works in the collection, colored reproductions of its works, touring the collection, and presenting touring exhibitions of other art. The foundation's indenture of trust stipulated that the paintings in the collection be kept "in exactly the places they are." In essence, the art had to hang on the walls exactly as Barnes prescribed with no variation.

Barnes died in 1951. Immediately the five-member board was faced with the challenge of how to generate enough revenues to keep the foundation operating. After a decade of legal challenges, in 1961 public access was expanded to two and a half days a week, with a limit of five hundred visitors per week. The waiting list was long. Visitors needed to make reservations by telephone at least two weeks in advance.

Faced with stagnant revenues, for decades the five board members "kicked the can down the road." Because the board was locked into the constrained conditions spelled out by the trust, there wasn't much strategic planning in progress.

In 1992, Richard H. Glanton, president of the foundation, reported that major infrastructure work had to be done, including major repairs to upgrade the mechanical systems. Also required were funds to maintain and preserve the works of art and improve security. Glanton realized that in order to raise the needed funds, they would have to break some terms of the indenture. He arranged for eighty-three Impressionist and post-Impressionist paintings to be sent on a world tour, which lasted from 1993 to 1995. He also loaned several works to other organizations. Groups opposed to these actions that broke the terms challenged Glanton in court, but they were unsuccessful.

The foundation also attempted to extend the number of hours the museum was open and to allow more visitors, but the governments of Merion and Montgomery County would not allow it to do so. To make matters worse, it was determined that there were financial irregularities in the running of the foundation. With all that was happening—the failing infrastructure, financial irregularities, and mounting legal expenses incurred because of court challenges—it was not surprising that the foundation's monetary situation worsened.

In 1998, the foundation hired Kimberly Camp as its first professional CEO, a position she held for seven years. During her successful tenure, she revived the foundation and generated support for a petition to move the Barnes to Philadelphia. In September 2002, the foundation petitioned the Montgomery County Orphans' Court to let the collection relocate to Center City, Philadelphia. They presented the case that if the struggling foundation was to survive, the public had to have more access to the collection and that nearby mass transit was necessary. In its brief to the court, the foundation explained that donors were hesitant to commit additional funds to the Barnes unless the gallery became more accessible to the public. The foundation also argued that in order to increase its fundraising potential, it needed to expand positions on the board of trustees from five (four of which were held by persons appointed by Lincoln University) to fifteen.

The court battle lasted two years and included an examination of the foundation's financial situation. Finally, in December 2004, Judge Stanley Ott ruled that the foundation could move from Merion to downtown Philadelphia. This was welcome news! Three charitable foundations—The Pew Charitable Trusts, the Lenfest Foundation, and the Annenberg Foundation—had each agreed to help the Barnes raise $150 million for a new building and endowment providing the move was approved by the court. To maintain the experience as Albert Barnes had intended, the Barnes Foundation pledged to reproduce Barnes's artistic arrangement of the artworks and other furniture within the new gallery.

However, Judge Ott's decision in 2004 was not the end of the story. The Friends of the Barnes Foundation and Montgomery County each filed briefs in Montgomery County Orphans' Court to reopen the hearings and challenge the move. They tried to convince the judge to reopen the case citing the changed circumstances in the County as the reason.

From the perspective of the role of the board in strategic planning, the key concept at play in the Barnes saga can be summarized best by this quote from a court document dated February 29, 2008, filed by Montgomery County in opposition to the move: "The Trustees of the Barnes Foundation have a continuing fiduciary obligation to adhere to the terms of the trust and to carry out the intent of the donor, which is paramount. Where circumstances arise which will allow the testator's clearly expressed intent to be followed, Trustees must follow it."

The Montgomery County motion referenced the December 13, 2004 ruling of the court, which said in part, "We...determined that the foundation was on the brink of financial collapse, and that the provision in Dr. Barnes' indenture mandating that the gallery be maintained in Merion was not sacrosanct, and could yield under the 'doctrine of deviation,' provided we were convinced the move to Philadelphia represented the least drastic modification of the indenture that would accomplish the donor's desired ends."

For decades, the challenge for the Barnes Foundation board had been to find the best path forward for the organization that represented the "least drastic modification of the indenture." It had become clear to the board that because of the constraints imposed by the gallery's location and the terms of Dr. Barnes's indenture, long-range strategic planning was a hopeless task. During the legal battles, the board's planning efforts were opposed by groups—among them the Friends of the Barnes Foundation and the civic government of Montgomery County—that continually insisted that there existed the means to generate sufficient revenues while keeping the gallery in its original Merion location. Fortunately for the foundation, on May 15, 2008, Judge Ott dismissed their requests due to lack of standing.

Construction of the new downtown Barnes Foundation building started in fall 2009 and was completed in May 2012. The galleries in the new facility replicate the originals in the Merion location in terms of scale, proportion, and configuration; however, the new venue contains more space to accommodate the foundation's art education program and its conservation department as well as a new retail shop and cafe. And just as importantly, the board is now able to make long-range strategic plans that are based in reality and have a reasonable chance of success.

This case is so important because it raises the question of the role of the board. From one viewpoint, the board's role is to preserve the institution and its assets exactly as the founders intended. The other perspective that eventually prevailed saw the board's role to be strategic; that it preserved a museum, and that details such as location, hours, and program are fungible in service of that purpose.

Once planning can feasibly happen and the mission is checked, boards often use planning processes to explore issues of capacity, growth, succession, capital improvements, diversified funding, and more. Increasingly, borrowing from best business practices, nonprofits are creating scorecards to report the data of their key performance indicators (KPISs) and track performance against monthly or quarterly targets as part of monitoring their planning process.

Once a plan is complete, the development director should lead the charge of creating a financial resource development strategy that will fund and support the desired plans. There are many plans made in nonprofit governance and management to chart the desired course of the organization. As Peter Drucker, the management consultant and thought leader whose works shaped modern business management, famously said (and I remind my clients of this all the time), *"Plans are only good intentions unless they immediately degenerate into hard work."*

In the next chapter, we'll take a closer look at turning plans into actions—how you can represent the organization to your friends, colleagues, and community. O

10

....

BEING AN AMBASSADOR AND A FRIENDRAISER

You give but little when you give of your possessions.
It is when you give of yourself that you truly give.

~ KAHLIL GIBRAN

Now that you've settled into your role as board member of the
Sunshine Charitable Foundation, you have become more confident
and more deeply involved with your board work. You are participating
during board meetings, and you have joined a working committee or two.
What is particularly gratifying is that you are seeing the positive effects of
both your individual efforts and the work of the board as a whole as it
supports the mission of the organization. Perhaps you've helped the
organization raise funds, launch a new program, or serve more people.
However you personally contribute, the feeling you are getting is
hopefully a good one.

Because you are comfortable working within the organization
(literally—in the building or on the campus), you are ready to step up to
the next level of involvement, which is to become an *ambassador* and a
friendraiser. These two words are used exactly as you might think. An
ambassador is someone who represents the organization in external
arenas: in the community, to other organizations, and to individual
prospective supporters and donors. A friendraiser is someone who actively
invites others to experience or get to know the nonprofit in various ways.

There are two types of ambassadors: passive and active.

THE PASSIVE AMBASSADOR

A passive ambassador is anyone who is part of the organization and who is identified as such in any public or external situation. It means that your name is usually on the website and letterhead, and you are associated publicly with the organization. To be a passive ambassador does not require you to do anything. You are not a salesperson. You are not knocking on doors and asking people for money. Many board members—perhaps you are one of them—simply do not enjoy being vocal about their activities. They are essentially more introverted and function best when they are well within their comfort zones. This is perfectly fine! Being a board member is a volunteer job, and it is supposed to be pleasant and rewarding, not torture.

But as a board member—even one who shuns the spotlight—you need to understand that your involvement with the organization is a matter of public record in your community, and that your actions, both as a voting board member and as a private citizen, will reflect upon the organization. Whether passive or active, every board member is part of the public relations team in the sense that your involvement, presence, values, and ethics reflect upon the organization itself.

There are obvious and crude ways where this can be seen. For example, a rape crisis center will not have on its board a misguided person who thinks women "invite" abuse (we've seen such people in the news recently). Such an individual who holds beliefs or values that are in conflict with the organization should not be associated with it and cannot possibly be an ambassador.

In a more commonplace example, if you are on the board of the City Art Museum and you attend a gallery opening for a hot new artist, you are representing the museum. Assuming you have a passion for art, your presence will act as a subtle validation of the museum's place in the art community. You have done this simply by showing up and being the gracious and refined person that you are.

THE ACTIVE AMBASSADOR

If you are more of an extroverted type who enjoys being a "connector," meeting new people, and even speaking in public, you may be comfortable as an active ambassador. As an active ambassador, you openly advocate on behalf of the organization and raise awareness about its mission and programs.

If it is a membership organization, such as a community center or museum, you might be part of the sales team that helps solicit new members. Your activities might include using social media to share a news article featuring your organization with your personal contacts, staffing a table at a community fair, or speaking about the organization at events. If your nonprofit is an advocacy organization, you may speak about the mission and efforts at community happenings, such as Rotary Club lunches or Chamber of Commerce events.

As an active ambassador, you'll be on the lookout for opportunities to talk about your nonprofit and to network. You do not have to follow up on each contact you make. You can—and should—pass the names along to appropriate staff of the nonprofit. Keep an eye out for these networking opportunities:

- Opportunities to showcase your nonprofit. This can be anywhere from neighborhood block parties to magazine spreads about volunteer opportunities.

- Contacts for memberships or programs. You may know someone who shares an interest in an upcoming education program or lecture or who may benefit from a family membership at your community center, theatre, performing arts organization, or museum.

- Contacts for volunteering. Many businesses don't always give cash donations to nonprofits, but instead they loan out their employees for a day or two every year for volunteer work. Other popular sources of volunteers include retired persons and people with young children who have chosen to stay home and not work full time, but want something to do outside the home a few days a week.

- Contacts who are community leaders and opinion makers. If you enjoy getting out and meeting new people, then you will easily mix at community events from political forums to garden lectures.

- Contacts for funding. These may include local businesses, foundations, and individuals. Most local banks have a set amount earmarked every year for community giving; if you get to know the bank president or a vice president, you can get your organization on the bank's radar screen. If you do not know any of the bank officers, join the local Chamber of Commerce, where banks are always well represented.

Let's say that you're not exactly an extrovert, but you feel as though you can take a more active role in representing the organization in your community. You are ready to step into one of the most important roles of any board member—that of *friendraising*.

FRIENDRAISING

Many people find it difficult to ask for money for their favorite cause—that is, to fundraise. Fundraising is an interesting combination of art and science, and not everyone can do it. You should never feel pressured to ask for money, and if it is not something you like to do, you should steer clear of it. This does not mean that you cannot make a significant contribution as a board member in other ways. In many respects, friendraising is just as important as fundraising, and it is something that just about any board member can do.

The essence of friendraising is that while it can be difficult to ask a friend or colleague to make a donation—to give something—it is easy and fun to *offer* them something as way to introduce the organization to them or deepen their involvement. Nearly every charitable organization has some sort of activity or event that is accessible to potential friends and donors. Art museums have exhibit openings. Symphonies and dance companies have performances. Hospitals have donor events or annual galas. Churches and synagogues have social and educational events and services. Environmental organizations have cleanup days.

The most common way to engage in friendraising is to simply invite a friend or colleague to accompany you to an event held by the organization. The key to making it work is that the organization does the selling. All you are doing is offering the opportunity for your friend to enjoy something. You are not putting yourself in the position of promoting the organization; you are just saying, "Come with me to the art opening (or lecture, or concert, or open house) and have fun." If your friend attends and has a good time, then terrific! You've made a positive connection. If your friend attends and isn't captivated, then there's no harm done, and no one's embarrassed.

An organization counts on its board to make introductions. Having made an introduction, you have every right to step aside and let the organization capitalize on the possibility that your friend or colleague may want to get more involved. This is the job of the professional staff—membership/sales, programming, and development. You should be willing to provide the development director with your friend's name and contact information as well as any special instructions that will affect the nature and frequency of contact made by the organization. If you believe, for example, that your friend will react negatively to being put on the organization's e-mail list, then you should make this clear. The number-one rule of donor cultivation is that the utmost tact and discretion must be used. Any and every interaction that your friend has with the organization must be 100 percent positive and pleasant. This is the tacit agreement that you have with the organization: you bring your friends, and the organization gives them the white-glove treatment.

A friend served on the board of a local art museum. It was a mid-sized organization with a budget of $2 million a year. One of the members of the board was a lovely woman named Rose. She was an antiques dealer, and her husband was a doctor. Rose was a shy and private individual. Although she attended every board meeting, she rarely spoke. Her quiet demeanor made it possible for you to think that she wasn't really engaged. But everyone noticed that whenever the museum had an opening or other big event, Rose would bring her cousin, whose name was Cynthia. (Rose's husband was never seen. We knew he existed, but art was not his thing.) We knew nothing about Cynthia, and little personal information was offered by either of the ladies.

After a few years of this, the museum announced a major capital campaign to build a new wing. The development department was looking for a leadership gift of $500,000. Suddenly, out of nowhere a check arrived in the mail for $500,000. The check was drawn on a private donor-directed foundation called the Windward Fund in care of a local law firm. No one had ever heard of the Windward Fund. After a bit of sleuthing, it was discovered that Rose's cousin Cynthia was its controlling donor. For the past several years Rose had been quietly bringing her cousin to museum events, and in her very low-key way had cultivated Cynthia. There was no pressure and no spotlight. When the time came that Cynthia felt that she could make a significant difference to the museum, she wrote the check.

Funny thing is, in terms of her relationship to the museum, nothing changed. While Cynthia did consent to attend the grand opening of the new wing, she didn't want her name put over the door. (She eventually consented to having the museum credit the Windward Fund in its annual report.)

Cynthia continued to show up every once in a while at openings and events, and wisely no one from the museum ever asked her to give another penny. Everyone knew that if Cynthia wanted to write another check, she would. And she did—every year thereafter, the Windward Fund made a nice gift of $5,000 to the annual appeal.

INVOLVEMENT LEADS TO INVESTMENT

In the nonprofit world, it is an old axiom that involvement leads to investment. It is a truism that should be reassuring to you, the friendraiser and ambassador. Why? Because you know intuitively that to approach someone like Cynthia too early and ask her for a donation would be off-putting and may even drive her away. It would seem crass. It would make you uncomfortable because you know deep down inside that the prospective donor does not yet have a real or lasting connection to the organization.

On the other hand, if someone like Cynthia has a chance to get to know the organization, see the passion that you and others have for it, and become comfortable with the mission, the staff, and the programs, it won't take much of an *ask* (yes, in the fundraising world, *ask* is a noun) to awaken the philanthropic spirit. People like to go where their personal values are reflected and where their contribution—of time, money, or expertise—will make a difference. By getting to know how their money will be spent, they come to believe that their contribution will make a difference.

The other thing to consider is that people generally do not enjoy saying no. It's embarrassing, and they assume that your feelings might be hurt by their refusal to write a check to the organization on whose board you serve. This is why involvement is the path to take. By opening the door to involvement, you give them the opportunity either to proceed ahead or to back away with no feelings hurt.

Here are two scenarios that will show you what I mean.

You serve on the board of the local symphony orchestra. You invite your friend Bill to a concert. He has never been and is happy to go. He seems to enjoy the concert. A few days later, you call Bill, and during your friendly chat you ask him how he enjoyed the evening and if he wants to be added to the symphony's e-mail list.

In the first scenario, he says, "I don't know... I'm awfully busy... I get a lot of spam in my inbox, and the e-mails might get deleted."

You say, "No problem. I understand." You decide to not mention the symphony again to Bill for a while, and you change the subject.

In the second scenario, he says, "Sure. I'd be happy to get symphony e-mails. I never realized how good the players are."

You say, "Okay, will do." And you make a note to send an invitation to Bill for the upcoming concert in the park. His involvement has begun.

These first overtures are low key, casual, and "weightless." No one is made to feel bad or embarrassed if they decline to get involved.

Remember that we're discussing your *individual* activities as a board member, not the broad mass-marketing efforts made by some big organizations. For example, you've seen those hard-sell ads on TV for animal-rescue organizations. They show a video of a poor suffering dog or kitten and then ask you for a donation. Or the Red Cross, which runs TV ads showing scenes of natural disasters followed by an appeal for donations. These are entirely different scenarios in which the "product" of the nonprofit—services to the afflicted—is "sold" like any other product. In such cases, the organization wants to pull at the heartstrings, and the viewers are made to feel badly if they do not contribute. It is a sales pitch made to strangers, and as a board member you are not required to get involved in anything like that. These are marketing campaigns, not traditional fundraising (or friendraising!).

As an active ambassador and friendraiser, here are just some of the ways that you can reach out and create a connection between the organization and your friends or colleagues:

- Create a personal list of your contacts that you seek to connect with the organization.

- If you have knowledge of a contact's interests or passion, have a chat with him or her to discover if the organization might be a good fit.

- Talk about your personal involvement and the organization's work over coffee or a meal.

- Forward e-mails about programs, events, and news.

- Use social media such as Facebook, Twitter, LinkedIn, and Instagram to share information and promote events.

- Make phone calls and include handwritten notes to event invitations.

- Invite them as your guests to a special event (e.g., to sit at your table at a gala).

- Bring them to educational programs.

- Invite them to go on a site visit.

- Ask them to volunteer together with you.

- Seek out advice relevant to their field or interests on behalf of the organization.

- Inquire about pro bono services.

After each of these engagements, it is critical to follow up and also to report back to your point of contact at the organization, whether it is the development director or the membership coordinator, so he or she can track the relationship as it progresses. Smart organizations will use some form of customer-relations management (CRM) database to organize the information.

As a board member who embraces being an ambassador and friendraiser, you will be most effective if you look, feel, and touch the mission and the people the organization serves. Get inspired and motivated! Let your heart be touched. Then you will tell a great story about your involvement and the organization and touch others.

Next I'll teach you how to have an impact story in your back pocket, ready to tell. ○

11

··

Storytelling

I've learned that people will forget what you said,
people will forget what you did, but people will never forget
how you made them feel.

~ MAYA ANGELOU

[Author's note: Examples in this chapter have been modified to respect client identities.]

As a board member, you are on the inside of the organization. You see the results of the organization's work. You feel the passion of the staff and volunteers. You are easily caught up in the excitement and energy.

As a friendraiser and ambassador, how do you convey that feeling to your friends and colleagues? How do you get them to feel the spirit and impact of the activities the way you do so they will want to get involved? You can answer that yourself by reading the two stories that follow and choosing which one would grab you and get your attention.

Story 1

The Northside Hospital, a nonprofit healthcare organization, serves 6,500 patients per year at our two cutting-edge facilities. Sixty percent of our patients are treated for some form of cancer, which is the focus of our practice. Of these, 50 percent are pediatric. Many of the patients are low income, and every year Northside Hospital subsidizes the treatment of low-income patients, especially children. In the previous fiscal year such subsidies totaled $3.2 million. The rate of subsidies has been growing at least 12 percent each year for the last five years. The average hospital stay is approximately two weeks, with outpatient therapy that may continue for a year or more. Our remission rate for pediatric cancer patients is one of the highest in the healthcare industry.

Story 2

Meet Suzy Smith. She's eight years old. When she was only six, she developed a rare form of liver cancer. Suzy's doctor told her parents, John and Lisa Smith, the grim news: Suzy might not live more than another year. Her parents rushed Suzy to Northside Hospital. Working closely with Northside's skilled pediatric cancer specialists, they created a plan of treatment for Suzy. After a two-week stay in the hospital—subsidized by Northside's generous Family Fund—Suzy was able to go home. After a year of outpatient treatment, Suzy was declared cancer free. "We cannot thank Northside Hospital enough," said Lisa Smith. "They saved our child's life and our family from financial ruin. Without the Family Fund, we would have had to sell our house to pay for treatment."

For the astute reader who counts words, these paragraphs are the same length—about 120 words each. The first paragraph is a dry recitation of facts and figures. It's informative, if you're interested in statistics. The second paragraph is the story of a little girl who had cancer and who is alive today thanks to Northside Hospital.

Which story would you rather tell a friend or colleague so that they will understand the mission and work of Northside Hospital?

THE POWER OF STORIES

When we need to use persuasion and influence to convince other people to support the organization, we tell stories. Stories have the power to move people to share our passion for the nonprofit more effectively than conveying dry stats and research alone to buttress our case. Through your involvement with the mission-focused work of the organization, you will most likely find yourself moved by the impact the nonprofit's work on its constituency. Whether it's witnessing the power of an after-school program's mentoring of an disadvantaged youth who stays in school and is the first person in his family to graduate from high school and go off to college, or seeing disabled adults participate joyfully in Olympics-style games, the impact of the nonprofit's work will move you.

To develop as a board member and in your role as ambassador, learning how to tell a story that makes the organization's work come to life is a very powerful and important tool. Stories inspire feeling, connection, and action. Stories allow us to make meaning of our lives and to share that meaning with others. We remember things when told in storytelling format much more than when we read text or hear a simple description.

Like the story of Suzy Smith, a well-crafted narrative evokes emotion, and it is not logic but emotion that drives charitable giving.

How to Use Storytelling

I am not saying that you need to become a master storyteller; I'm sure you don't need that kind of pressure! But you should understand how to relate the good works of the organization to a friend or colleague in a way that strikes a personal chord. When you engage someone in a conversation about the organization, it is a good idea to have thought about these questions in advance:

• Who are we as an organization?

• Why do we do what we do?

• Who benefits from our work?

- Why does the organization deserve support (i.e., time, talent, influence, and money) from prospective friends and donors?

- How can I illustrate how we provide a much-needed service that enhances the community?

In the example of Northside Hospital, you could recite a bunch of statistics to answer the last question. But the personal story of Suzy Smith is far more powerful.

Here's another example of a compelling story.

The Student Stars provides after-school programs that keep children safe and help them succeed in sports, school, and life. A young immigrant boy named Jose Martinez lived in a Los Angeles neighborhood known for pervasive gang violence. When Jose entered the Student Stars program, he spoke little English and seemed destined for a life on the margins. He stuck with the program, earned his high-school diploma with high honors, and was accepted at Harvard University. Four years later he graduated with a degree in engineering. Jose credits Student Stars and says that having positive adults who kept him safe after school, taught him academic and life skills, and exposed him to the college process were the major factors in his ability to succeed.

TIPS FOR EFFECTIVE STORYTELLING

- Make it interesting, motivational, and memorable.

- Draw the listener in with everyday language and emotions.

- Aim for the heart and strike an emotional chord.

- Wrap the story around a compelling character.

- Cause the listener to think about what his or her own family might have in common—or had in common at one time—with the people served by the organization.

- Remember basic story structure—a beginning, a middle, and an end! You want to feel like the story came to resolution, or completion. If you can, build a surprise.

- Keep it short—one or two minutes. Your story should be a quick sketch. Make it easy on both yourself and your listener.

- Be truthful.

A PUBLIC STORY OF SELF

"Stories allow us to express our values not as abstract principles, but as lived experiences," said Marshall Ganz of Harvard University, who came to national prominence as the organizer for then-Senator Barack Obama's 2008 presidential election campaign. "They have the power to move others."

When you do public work, you have a responsibility to offer a public account of who you are, what you do, and where you hope to lead. A good public story is drawn from challenges you faced, choices you made, and outcomes you experienced.

According to Ganz, who as of this writing still teaches the course entitled "Public Narrative: Self, Us, Now" at Harvard's John F. Kennedy School of Government, public narrative is a leadership art composed of three elements: a story of self, a story of us, and a story of now.

The Story of Self

According to the Harvard professor, "A story of self communicates who I am: my values, my experience, why I do what I do." It tells why you lead. Your personal narrative gives others insight into your values, why you have chosen to act, what people can expect from you, and what they can learn from you.

Why were you called to do what you do? Why do you volunteer or work for this organization? What motivates you? Why do you believe in the organization?

The Story of Us

A story of us communicates who we are: our shared values, our shared experience, and why we do what we do. What has the community been called to do? What is its shared purpose, goal, or vision?

The Story of Now

A story of now articulates the present as a moment of challenge, choice, and hope. What action does the mission require you to do right here, right now?

As a campaign strategy, Ganz postulated that campaign workers who approached potential voters needed to be able to quickly establish a personal relationship with the voter, and the way to do this was to tell their story of self. Then, the overarching story of us connected the values and interests of the campaign worker and voter with candidate President Obama.

Here's a story of self that leads to the broader story of us.

The mission of Lincoln College is to empower and educate young women to build and reshape their world in whatever way their passions lead them. Missy, a high school graduate from across the country, was excited to be accepted at Lincoln. At the first parents' weekend, her parents asked Missy if she had made the right decision. Missy replied yes; coming to Lincoln was the best decision of her life because *finally* she could speak up and be heard in class. Her parents were shocked to find out that at the expensive private high school that Missy had attended, the teachers more often called on the smartest boys. Even the boys had agreed.

Missy's parents were grateful to Lincoln for encouraging their daughter to find her voice and use it and for nurturing the unique gifts inside of her.

Why would this story matter, and to whom?

This story resonates with parents who want the very best for their children's educations. It would matter to any high-school student—male or female—who wants to contribute but feels overwhelmed or overlooked. It would matter to anyone—male or female—who at one time felt marginalized or invisible and wanted to find his or her voice.

Few organizations can be all things to all people. In business, there's something called the *unique selling proposition*. This is what differentiates your business or product from that of your competitors. Perhaps your product or service is lower in price, has more features, is available in more colors, or carries a longer warranty.

The above story describes Lincoln College's unique selling proposition: A one-of-a-kind institution where female students are given an environment where they are valued and can grow, as students and as leaders. Not every female high-school graduate will connect with this proposition. But many will—and Lincoln will attract an abundance of candidates who are a great fit for the school. Potential donors who empathize with Missy and her story will want to learn more about the school and how it can change the lives of its students—and how they can be a part of that.

As a member of the board of the Sunshine Charitable Foundation, what is your personal story? What is it about your experiences in life that drew you to the organization? After all, there must have been a time in your life when you didn't know much about the Sunshine Charitable Foundation. How did you discover it? What about its work resonated with you and made you want to get involved?

Consider John, who is an artist living in Boston. John creates paintings that are abstract and very challenging, and it isn't easy for him to find galleries or venues that will show his work. On a whim, he sent some images of his work to the Coolidge Art Association (CAA), a nonprofit arts organization. The CAA was presenting a juried exhibition that was open to anyone wishing to submit work. A few weeks later, the CAA told John that not only had his work been accepted into the exhibition, but that the juror for the CAA, a prominent local museum director, had given John's painting one of the prizes.

"I thought that any art association that welcomed my work was worth investigating," said John. "So I started attending the openings and getting to know the people there." After a few months, the association's executive director (who was a board member and a one-person leadership development committee) asked John if he wanted to join the board. He agreed. After serving on the board for two years, he was asked to become the board president. He served for two years as the president, which was unusual because most of the previous board presidents had served terms of just one year.

"Most of the twenty members of the board of the CAA were artists," said John. "Serving on a board with a bunch of artists is like herding cats. For some reason, I was a good fit as president. I guess I was adept at herding cats. And to think that it all started when I sent in a few images of my work for an exhibition. CAA gave my work a platform and I wanted to do that for other artists."

You, too, probably have a personal story of how you made the decision to get involved with the organization. People whom you meet deserve to hear it—it may touch something within them and spur them into action. Organizational and personal stories are an important tool for our next subject, fundraising. O

12

THE FUNDAMENTALS OF FUNDRAISING

We make a living by what we get;
we make a life by what we give.

~ SIR WINSTON CHURCHILL

Having grown comfortable with the process of friendraising for the Sunrise Charitable Foundation, you are ready to go up to the next level: *fundraising.* This is great. Because of all of the perceived challenges of serving on a board, fundraising is perhaps the task that most often strikes fear into the hearts of perfectly capable people who would otherwise make terrific board members.

It is a fact of life that nonprofit organizations need money to operate. They need it to hire staff and they need to pay for utilities, insurance, and office supplies—all the "stuff" that it takes to keep the doors open and the lights turned on and run their programs or services. They may need money for big projects, like new technology or buildings or endowments.

Depending upon the financial structure of the organization, to meet its revenue goals an organization may do very little fundraising, or it may be a constant, never-ending activity.

Many board members are enthusiastic about fundraising—they enjoy the social aspect and feel a deep sense of fulfillment from their efforts. On the other hand, some find it as enjoyable as a root canal.

During a fundraising training session that I led at a mid-size nonprofit, a board member lamented that he hated asking people for money. One of his colleagues chimed in that she wished that fundraising weren't a board responsibility.

Both seemed shocked when I told them not to do it. *Don't fundraise.* Everyone looked at me as if I had lost my mind. Wasn't I there to give training on solicitation?

Here's the truth: every board has a choice. As fiduciaries, board members are responsible for both the *expense* side and the *revenue side* of the organization's annual budget. If the revenue in the form of dues, membership dollars, fees for services, rentals, or for-profit ventures can meet the organization's costs, then by all means, do not fundraise.

However, once you budget to spend more than you generate from revenue—whether to cover costs of services, to improve programs, to invest in staff or infrastructure, to serve more people, or to expand your reach—the organization must seek philanthropic support and investment. You can hire excellent development staff, but it is legally and ultimately the board's responsibility as fiduciary to balance the budget.

The good news for boards is that fundraising does not have to be dreadful. Quite the opposite. The bottom line is that fundraising is something all board members should know about; however, it may not be necessary for all to be involved with it beyond making their own gift and, hopefully, making introductions, sharing their own networks, and attending events. One reason that my job is personally rewarding is because I teach people how to raise money and to feel comfortable doing so. Believe it or not, many of the board members I have trained have changed their initial feelings about it and now enjoy solicitation. Giving is an expression of values, and soliciting is an invitation for people to demonstrate their values and do something meaningful.

Let's assume that the Sunrise Charitable Foundation does not have enough earned income and investment income to meet its annual goals as reflected in its expenses. Like many charitable nonprofits, Sunrise must depend upon donations to make up the difference.

THE DIFFERENCE BETWEEN FRIENDRAISING AND FUNDRAISING

In its most simple and fundamental terms, there is only one difference between friendraising and fundraising:

Asking.

When you friendraise, you don't ask. You *give.* You invite your friend or colleague to an event. You show him or her a good time and share with your friend the wonderful work of the organization. You ask nothing in return.

When you fundraise, you *ask* for a donation. At the appropriate time, you make the subtle pivot from giving and you ask them for financial support. That's the difference.

Fortunately, in a well-organized nonprofit like the Sunrise Charitable Foundation, the mechanism for fundraising is both comprehensive and deliberate. As a board member, you'll never be put in the awkward position of asking someone for money when the odds of success have not been carefully calculated to be in your favor. As I've mentioned before, if everyone does his or her job correctly, an "ask" will never seem abrupt or pushy. The prospect may decline or give less than you hoped but should never be offended.

In a large organization with a full staff, there will be many people—employees, consultants, and volunteers—who participate in fundraising activities. Let's take a look at them and how their efforts work together to make your job easier.

Development Committee

At the board level, the development committee is charged with meeting the annual budget goal for donated funds. It is important because the committee's mission speaks to the very essence of the organization's ability to survive, and its activities may require the coordination of many departments. The development committee works closely with the entire board and professional staff. Here are the typical members of the development team.

Professional Staff

- Executive director or CEO

- Development vice president, director, or manager

- Marketing/communication manager

- Finance manager

Board Members

- President and vice president(s)

- Development committee chair

- Development committee members

Consultants (as necessary)

- Campaign consultants (annual fund, capital campaign, endowment campaign)

- Fundraising training consultant

- Grant writer

The development committee may need to juggle two or more major initiatives at one time, such as the annual fund and the annual fundraising gala. To do this, there may exist development subcommittees, where each one is dedicated to one of the major initiatives.

The Vice President of Development

This key individual on the committee is the highest-ranked paid staff member who is directly responsible for development. Depending on the size of the organization, the title may be vice president of development, director of development, or development manager.

In a large organization, the vice president of development is responsible for a wide range of initiatives and revenue streams. He or she serves as a key leadership team member and an active participant in making strategic decisions affecting the organization. The vice president of development must forge new relationships to build the nonprofit's impact, visibility, and financial resources. He or she must design and implement a comprehensive plan for developing key external alliances by cultivating individual and philanthropic support. Revenues may come from sources including but not limited to the solicitation of individual gifts, federal and state grants, special events, and corporate and foundation support.

The vice president of development must broaden the donor base or pipeline, work closely with the board of directors, and support board members as they assume active fundraising roles. At most nonprofits it is expected that revenues raised will increase year-over-year as the vice president of development systematically and effectively strengthens the organization's overall fundraising capacity.

It is important for you as a board member to understand that the vice president of development (and indeed all of the development staff) is a behind-the-scenes worker. When securing gifts from individuals and corporations, the development staff will frequently lay the groundwork but not actually make the ask. That last critical step is often performed by the executive director or a board member (like you!). Because they are not in the spotlight, development professionals often seem disposable. This can be a huge misconception. More than one shortsighted, small nonprofit has laid off the development director in the misguided belief that the salary could be saved and the work could be picked up by volunteers and the executive director. When reality hits, it is too late and donations plummet. Another big mistake is for the board to arbitrarily increase the fundraising goals without adding to the development staff. This is when your development director will start looking for another place to work.

Unlike staff members such as program people, who, when they're hired can usually hit the ground running, a development person's effectiveness takes time to hit its stride. An organization cannot hire a new vice president of development and expect an overnight jump in donations. It can take years for relationships to develop and plans to mature. High turnover in the development office is a bad thing, and the organization needs to nurture and support its development staff.

DONATION SOURCES

Nonprofits can earn money just like any other businesses—by selling services, charging rents, collecting tuition, and managing investments. As a board member, these revenue streams are part of the annual budget and within your responsibility.

This chapter of the book is devoted to what makes a nonprofit different—its ability to solicit donations that, to the donor, are most often tax deductible. As I mentioned earlier, while it is possible that a nonprofit may not require donations and fundraising, it is highly unlikely. Most nonprofits require donated income to meet their budgetary requirements. A broad income base with multiple revenue streams is generally preferable to depending upon just a few sources.

Here are many of the sources of donated income that you might find in the annual budget or the development plan and the types of gifts or grants they might give.

Individuals

• Tribute gifts, in memory of a loved one or in honor of someone at a milestone

• Annual appeal or annual fund (same thing)

• Major gifts to a campaign

• Planned giving or bequests

• Crowdfunding (funding a project by raising many small amounts of money from a large number of people, especially via the Internet)

• Memberships that exceed the price of regular membership (e.g., as sustaining or benefactor members)

Special Events
(These will be discussed further in Chapter 14.)

• Annual gala

• Auctions

• Community walks or runs (for hunger, cancer, etc.)

• Golf tournaments

• Poker tournaments

Foundations

- Large private foundations

- Family foundations

- Donor-advised funds

- Community foundations

- Corporate foundations

Government

- Local, state, and federal agencies that make grants

Corporations

- Corporate sponsorships and support

- Cause marketing

- In-kind gifts of products, materials, or expertise

As a board member, when each of the funding sources are presented and discussed throughout the year, you will almost certainly be asked to review your list of contacts within the community and to advise the development department if you know someone who could be a prospective donor or participant.

For example, charity golf tournaments are becoming increasingly popular. They're typically scheduled for Mondays, the slow days on golf courses. The nonprofit organization pays a fee to the golf course and then sells slots in the tournament. Local businesses are tapped to provide prizes. The participants—the golfers—are local businesspeople who are happy to hit the links on a Monday and schmooze with their local colleagues.

When the vice president of development announces plans for the first annual Sunrise Charitable Foundation Golf Tournament, you'll be asked to suggest someone—or a company—you personally know who might want to participate or, better yet, to become a sponsor.

Let's say that the vice president of the local bank (we'll call it First City Bank) happens to be the person who handles your company's loan account. You are Emily Jones's client, and your company is a very good customer of First City Bank.

The development department will invite every bank in town to participate in the golf tournament, including First City Bank. But it's always better to have an inside connection. It is always better to make a personal invitation. That's why the vice president of development, who is in charge of coordinating the "asks," will say to you, "Would you mind personally delivering the golf tournament package to Emily Jones at First Bank? You don't have to create the package; we'll do that for you. All you have to do is call Emily and ask if you can stop by her office. When you see her, just say that we're presenting a terrific golf tournament, and we'd love it if First City Bank chose to be a sponsor."

You don't have to pressure Emily for an answer. All you need to do is have a friendly chat and put the offer on her desk. No sweat! If the bank can't do it, it's no embarrassment to either party. If the bank decides to participate, you'll go on record as having made the connection. At the golf tournament, the development staff will make sure that you are present to greet the group from First City Bank. (Remember what I said earlier about the development staff acting as facilitators behind the scenes? This is a good example.)

When you make your visit to the bank, if you want to be accompanied by a member of the development team, that's perfectly fine, and not at all uncommon.

If you want to take a more active role and work with Emily Jones to determine the level of sponsorship that the bank is most comfortable with, you can do that too. The key is to keep the manager of this project— the development department—fully apprised of your progress.

In the private access area of our website, we've included another bonus for you—a simple Solicitation Checklist to help keep your organization on track with solicitations. Go to www.fridmanstrategies.com (password: **ONBOARD**).

RESTRICTED AND NON-RESTRICTED GIFTS

Before I conclude the fundamentals of fundraising, it's important that you understand that the *intention* of the donor can make a difference to the organization.

The law recognizes that donors can specify that their gift to the organization fall into one of two categories.

Non-restricted gifts can be used by the organization for any purpose, including general operating expenses, such as staff salaries and utility bills. Nonprofits love non-restricted (or unrestricted) gifts because they come with no strings attached. The funds can be used for whatever purpose the executive director or finance manager deems appropriate. Generally, gifts to the annual fund are non-restricted.

Restricted gifts are accepted by the organization with the pledge by the organization that the gift will support the budget area specified by the donor. This happens when a donor wants to support a specific program or budget line of the organization. If the nonprofit accepts the gift, it must keep the funds in a designated account whose balance reflects the total number of gifts put into that account.

Here are some examples of restricted gifts:

- A grant made to support a museum exhibition (funds must be assigned to the exhibition budget)

- A donation made to the endowment fund, which is always separate from the organization's operating account

- A gift made to support a specific program for education or travel

With the exception of endowment funds, which are truly distinct from operating funds, you could make the argument that restricted gifts are simply an illusion. Why? Let's say a museum exhibition is budgeted to cost $500,000. Lucy Williams donates $50,000 as a restricted gift to the exhibition. Now the exhibition budget has $50,000 more dollars than anticipated. This means that the museum needs to dedicate only $450,000 of its operating budget to the exhibition. The other $50,000 can be used somewhere else. Money is fungible.

A shell game? Perhaps. But when Lucy Williams sees the exhibition and her name on a plaque on the wall outside the door, she'll feel pretty good about her contribution.

In the next chapter, we'll look in more detail at major gifts and fundraising campaigns—how they work and your role in them. O

13

···

MAJOR GIFTS AND CAMPAIGNS

It is every man's obligation to put back into the world at least the equivalent of what he takes out of it.

~ ALBERT EINSTEIN

If Chapter 12 is the 100 level of fundraising, this is the 200-level course!

As a member of the board of the Sunrise Charitable Foundation, it's possible that you could serve for years without dipping your toe into the major gifts and campaigns segment of fundraising.

It's not that you won't do your share of fundraising. You may even be responsible for bringing in significant levels of cash and gifts every year. But there's a difference between everyday giving and the jump into major gifts. This difference is most significant when viewed from the point of view of the donor. Here's what I mean.

Among fundraising professionals, it's an axiom that individuals make annual gifts from their own operating accounts—their checkbooks. These gifts include the following:

• The annual fund or annual appeal

• Membership fees

- Tickets and sponsorships for charity events, such as the gala dinner dance or the golf tournament

The amounts are not necessarily small; a person of high net worth may be able to write a five-figure check from his or her household account. People who are philanthropically active budget for each year's gift(s), and that's what their giving program is—part of their household budget. It is a choice they make. Most philanthropic individuals support a chosen handful of charities—a church or temple, a hospital, a museum, a soup kitchen, an alma mater—and plan on giving a certain amount every year. The tax advantages are attractive, but a tax deduction may not be the most compelling reason they make donations. They give because they support their chosen organizations' missions and programs.

The same applies to corporate giving programs, which are budgeted every year.

When a nonprofit organization plans its budget for the upcoming year, it is because of this regularity of giving that the development department can look at the past record of individual and corporate giving and get a good estimate of how much they can raise.

Family status can make a difference. If the development director learns that Joe and Patty Jones are going through a contested divorce, he or she may make a note that Patty's customary $1,000 annual appeal gift may not be coming this year. In the database of donors, the couple may be flagged "Do not solicit." It's all part of the *donor-centric* approach—the last thing you want to do is ask for money from someone who's in divorce court.

MAJOR GIFTS

It's a good idea to remember that individuals and families often make annual gifts to a specific area or campaign in the organization that they support. For example, Paula Williams serves on the board of the regional Valley Wildlife Preserve. Like most nonprofits, each year the Preserve has an annual appeal. The goal of the annual appeal is $500,000. Each of the twenty members of the board makes an annual appeal gift; the average size of each member's gift is $2,000.

Paula Williams and her husband jointly give $500 to the annual appeal. They both work in finance, and at first glance their level of giving seems, well, paltry. Couldn't they give more? Actually, they do. Paula happens to be co-chair of the annual fundraising gala. To its donors, the gala offers sponsorship levels: Diamond ($10,000), Gold ($5,000), Silver ($2,500), and Bronze ($1,000). Each sponsorship level comes with benefits, such as free tickets, an ad in the program, or admission to an exclusive cocktail reception. Paula and her husband are always Diamond Sponsors, a privilege for which they pay $10,000. (Because they receive tangible benefits, they cannot deduct the entire amount from their federal income taxes, the way they could for a gift to the annual appeal. The Preserve states that the value of the goods and services they have received at the Diamond level is $2,000; therefore, they can deduct only $8,000 from their taxes.)

With some justification, Paula believes that her $10,000 sponsorship gift puts her and her husband near the top of the annual giving list, and she's probably right. That's why she makes a token gift to the annual appeal.

Paula and her husband pay for their sponsorship out of their household checking account, through a donor-advised fund or through a family foundation. A donor-advised fund is a charitable giving vehicle administered by a public charity created by organizations, families, or individuals to manage their charitable donations. To participate, a donating individual or organization opens an account in the fund and deposits cash, securities, or other financial instruments. They surrender ownership of the funds in the account, but retain control over how their account is invested and how it distributes money to charities. However they source the funds, their gift is something they plan on every year.

A major gift is something that requires a higher level of planning or arranging. The difference between cyclical annual giving and a major gift is that for most individuals and corporations, a major gift comes not from the normal operating account but from capital.

This means that to make a major gift of, say, $100,000, Paula and her husband will have to sell some stock or other assets. This requires some real planning on their part because assets produce other assets; once you sell an asset and give away the money, it is not coming back. It is true that there will be some tax benefits to a large gift (Paula and her husband, like you, should consult a tax professional before making any large gift to a charity), but a really big gift can impact their lifestyle. It may require a choice—it might be that other charitable giving will be cut back that year or that Paula and her husband will postpone adding a wing to their own home until next year.

Major gifts are not made every year. There are occasions when donors will step up and contribute to an exceptional project. Let's have a look at when this might happen.

Capital Campaigns

As a board member of the Sunrise Charitable Foundation, let's say that you've been hearing discussion about the Foundation building a new wing. The current facility is outdated, too small, and cannot accommodate the growth that is outlined in the Foundation's long-range strategic plan. More program and administrative space is needed, and a restaurant and gift shop would be welcome additions. There is enough room on the property to build, but the Foundation is also eyeing a building to acquire and renovate.

At a board meeting, the president formally announces that the Foundation intends to explore the feasibility of a capital campaign to build a new wing.

"Feasibility" is the key word. Remember, the first rule of capital fundraising is that you never announce a capital campaign unless you're 99 percent certain that you'll reach the goal. Until you are certain, the campaign is not publicly discussed.

How can the organization be certain? The first step is with a *feasibility study.*

Generally, a feasibility study is conducted by an impartial outside consultant. By "outside," I mean literally from out of the orbit of the institution. It is better if the people who are doing the study do not have personal relationships with potential donors or the board.

Here is the basic project time line:

1. The Sunrise Charitable Foundation hires Apex Consultants to manage the feasibility study of the New Wing Project.

2. The first job is to figure out how much needs to be raised to build the new wing. Of course, everyone knows that initial estimates are always too low, but after consulting a builder and an architect, a figure is set at $5 million for design, construction, and ongoing maintenance. A rough rendering of the new wing is produced, along with a description.

3. The next step is to produce a pyramid of gifts. In table form, the pyramid will look like this:

Capital Campaign Sample Pyramid of Gifts

AMOUNT	NUMBER	TOTAL
$500,00 wing-naming gift	1	$500,000
$250,000	4	$1,000,000
$100,000	10	$1,000,000
$50,000 to $99,999	20	$1,000,000
$10,000 to $49,999	50	$500,000
$5,000 to $9,999	100	$500,000
$1,000 to $4,999	200	$200,000
Up to $999	300	$300,000

The pyramid consists of gifts of various sizes. The total must be $5 million. There will be many small gifts and fewer large ones. The pyramid shows the hypothetical number of gifts and amounts needed to reach $5 million.

4. Here's where you, the Sunrise board member, can get involved. The board president now asks for board members who want to serve on the campaign feasibility committee. The committee includes the president, the executive director, the development director, the representative from Apex Consulting, and a selection of board members who are well connected in the community.

You raise your hand and volunteer to join.

5. The next challenge is to determine whether or not the organization's current pool of donors is capable of filling all the slots in the gift pyramid. It is extremely important that at this critical stage, wishful thinking is *not* part of the process. At the conclusion of its research, Apex Consultants must provide Sunrise with the cold, hard facts: either the donor pool is sufficient, or it isn't. More than one capital campaign has been quietly

terminated or postponed at this stage because the donor pool just wasn't deep enough.

Meetings of the feasibility committee may be held offsite, perhaps in the home of a board member. Because sensitive personal information is being discussed, the utmost discretion must be observed. The goal of the meetings is to produce the *prospect list*. This is a list of potential high-level donors to the campaign. It is highly confidential.

The manager from Apex Consultants will organize and manage the prospect list, which is created by open discussion. Here's how.

To get started, the Sunrise development director passes out the organization's confidential list of all its major donors dating back five years. The list may include anyone who has given more than $5,000 (total) in any single year, for any reason. It will include individuals, corporations, and foundations.

Let's say that when all the names are compiled, the Sunrise list of its major donors totals one hundred individuals, companies, and foundations. The highest annual gift has been $250,000. This fact alone is a positive sign—the numbers are in the ballpark, and for the campaign to acquire a leadership gift of $500,000 may not be out of the question.

Now it's simply a matter of going down the names on the list, one by one. The chair of the feasibility committee will start the discussion.

"The first name is Jennifer Adams," says the chair. "She's been a donor every year for the past five years, and she consistently gives $10,000 a year. Does anyone personally know Jennifer?"

You raise your hand. "I know Jennifer. She serves on the hospital board with me. Two years ago she gave the hospital $100,000 for a new MRI machine."

"That's good," says the development director as he makes a note on the list.

"I know Jennifer too," says another board member. "Her husband was just named partner at his law firm. They handled the big auto recall lawsuit."

"Even better," says the development director as he makes another note. "So what do we think? Should we put her down for $100,000?"

Of course, this is sheer speculation, but when you're doing a feasibility study, you have no other choice. Remember, this is all being done in confidence.

"Okay," says the chair. "Next on the list is Joseph Ames. He gives $5,000 a year. That's it. No one ever sees him. He never comes to the annual gala. Does he have resources?"

"I see him around town," says a board member. "He drives an old Land Rover."

Judy, another board member, raises her hand. "My brother works at the law firm that handles the Ames family trust. Believe me, Joseph Ames has big money."

"Big money?" someone asks. "Like, how *big*?"

"Like big," says Judy. "The Ames family trust very quietly funds significant projects, many of them overseas. That's why you never hear about it. If Joseph Ames were so inclined, he could pay for the entire five-million-dollar project through the family trust."

"Very interesting," says the development director as he furiously makes notes.

And so it goes. It may take more than one meeting, but eventually every name on the list has been discussed. The Apex consultant takes this information, continues to prospect the potential donors, and tallies up the numbers. If the results look promising, he will recommend going to the next step.

6. The evidence suggests that the pool of donors is deep enough to support the campaign. This is when the consultant from Apex really swings into action. His next task is to interview a select number of potential donors. He wants to get their confidential and candid opinions about the Sunrise Charitable Foundation and the proposal to build a new wing. The appointments are set up through the development office. The consultant will visit the donors at their homes or offices and spend fifteen

or twenty minutes talking with each one. If the prospect's attitude towards Sunrise and the capital campaign is positive, he will ask them at what level they *might* support the project and will note their response.

7. When the interviews are complete, the Apex consultant will type up a brief report. It will state how many prospects were interviewed and include a sample of their statements. Most significantly, the report will state how many gifts and at what amounts may be expected from the group. The report will not include names. The statements provided by the interviewees are absolutely confidential.

The Apex consultant will deliver his or her report to the development committee. The full board will review it. Let's assume that the report indicates that it will be possible to raise $5 million from the one hundred names on the list. The board then votes to begin a quiet capital campaign.

During the *quiet* phase, pledges are secured from major donors. The campaign is not discussed in public, and there are no press releases.

Asking for Money

Now the campaign shifts gears, and it is time to start asking for donations. There are two ways that as a board member you can become involved.

First, you can personally ask a prospect for a gift. At the feasibility study meeting you said that you knew Jennifer Adams. At the next confidential meeting of what is now called the capital campaign committee, the prospect list is reviewed again. The campaign chair recalls that you said you know Jennifer Adams. Does anyone else know Jennifer as well as you? The chair turns to you and asks if you would be willing to contact Jennifer and discuss the campaign with her.

You might decline, for whatever reason.

Or you might say, "Of course, I'd be happy to. I'll give her a call tomorrow. I'll invite her out for coffee."

How you choose to approach Jennifer depends upon your relationship with her. You may be comfortable enough with her to simply say to her, "Hi, Jennifer. I'd like to run an idea past you. You know the Sunrise Charitable Foundation? Yes—they do wonderful work. As you may know, I'm on the board. We're thinking about building a new wing. It's desperately needed! Can we get together sometime to chat about it?"

Jennifer is no novice; she knows why you're calling! But it's okay, because there's no pressure. Jennifer can say, "I'd love to have coffee, but I'm not sure I can help with the Sunrise project. My husband and are up to our necks funding the new operating room at the hospital. But it would be lovely to see you."

You can put that down as a qualified "no." Or perhaps a "maybe."

Jennifer might also say, "That sounds lovely. I've heard so many good things about Sunrise. When do you want to get together?"

You can put Jennifer down as a *possible* donor.

When you meet Jennifer, if the vibe is positive, you'll hand her the Sunrise Capital Campaign packet that has been prepared by the development office. In the packet is the full-color sketch of the new wing, financial information, and the gift pyramid.

The text of the materials will provide a brief overview of the project. It will also present one or more stories.

Yes—*stories*. As we saw in Chapter 11, personal stories of how the organization has benefitted real people are very important. They bring to life the impact of the organization's work on the community. They highlight the necessity for expanding the organization's services, and the only way to do this is by building a new wing. Jennifer—and every potential donor—must feel the emotional pull of the project and see for themselves how it will improve lives.

If you are not comfortable with a direct "ask" of your friend Jennifer, it is not a problem. Many people are not comfortable asking others for money. There is a very effective alternative. Once the campaign goes public, you can host a get-together at your home, where someone from the campaign will give an informal chat about the project. The development office will coordinate the invitations; all you have to do is provide your home and gracious hospitality. Because the campaign is now public, there's no pretense; everyone who accepts your invitation will know the purpose of the gathering.

At such events, stories are extremely powerful. Here are some examples of how stories can be told:

- Soup kitchen: A PowerPoint slideshow presented by the development director highlighting how the soup kitchen feeds low-income clients

- Opera company: A song performed live by a singer whose big professional break came as the result of being hired by the company

- Conservation society: A presentation about how the society has recently saved wetlands from destruction

- Temple: A talk by the rabbi, who describes how the original temple has grown too small for the growing number of members

- Educational organizations: A speech by a current student or alum and/or performance of a skit, song, or dance routine by a group of students

Informal home get-togethers represent a good opportunity to spread the word about the good works of the organization as well as present the specific case for the capital expansion. All you have to do is play the role of the gracious host; you do not have to ask anyone for money. The development staff can handle that later.

Training

In a capital campaign, the role of the board is critical. Board members will be asked not only to make at least a token gift to show 100 percent board support but also to provide names of potential donors and to do whatever else they can to assist the campaign.

To increase the board's comfort level and to give the board members confidence in their roles as ambassadors, many organizations provide training for board members as the campaign begins. This may be anything from an evening session at the organization's facility led by the development director to a full-blown weekend retreat led by a professional consultant. You may even want to volunteer to host a weekend afternoon training session at your home. I've led trainings at the beginning of campaigns. Such sessions can spell the difference between a campaign that soars and one that sputters along and never gets off the ground.

If your organization is planning a major fundraising campaign and you are not confident in your ability to make a strong contribution, go to your board president and urge him or her to arrange for training. It will be well worth the minimal expense.

Going Public

If it is successful, the quiet phase of the campaign continues until a substantial number of major pledges have been secured that add up to at least half of the total goal. So if the goal is $5 million, then Sunrise will need to have at least $2.5 million in pledges before it goes public. The total may or may not include the big leadership gift; these often take more time to arrange.

At this point, you may be wondering, "Are these pledges legally binding?"

This is a very complex legal area. Courts have shown a willingness to enforce pledges, especially when some sort of consideration is involved, such as when a charity will name a building after a donor in exchange for a pledge. To further complicate matters, nonprofits are required by the Financial Accounting and Standards Board to report pledges on their accounting statements as part of their assets and resources.

While a pledge may be interpreted as a legally binding contract, most nonprofits are reluctant to take legal action to collect pledges because it is an expensive process and because if you sue a donor, you have burned that bridge forever. Most charities expect some donor "shrinkage" and write off unfulfilled pledges.

Once the total of pledged gifts hits one-half of the goal, the campaign is publically launched with great fanfare. The big donations "thermometer" is often mounted on the wall, tours are given of the proposed building site, meetings are held in people's homes, and speeches are given at Rotary Club luncheons. If all goes well, by the time the target deadline is reached—which might be as short as a year or as long as five years—the funding goal is met or exceeded, and construction begins.

Major campaigns can take many years to build and finally close because individuals and foundations often need several years to plan for and sometimes pay for their gifts. Your friend Jennifer may say to you, "We can't possibly consider a major gift until the operating room at the hospital has been built and dedicated. That should be sometime next year. Then we'll be able to talk about Sunrise." This is a very good sign! It means that Jennifer and her husband are interested in contributing, and patience is what is required now. Likewise, foundations often work on annual cycles, and it simply takes time for them to analyze and approve major gifts.

There's also the *bystander* effect. Not infrequently, individuals who can make major gifts wait until the organization can demonstrate that it has deep support for the project. Few big donors are willing to be the first to make a pledge. And many foundations require that their gift be matched, not necessarily by single gifts of equal size but by the total.

A positive outcome of the bystander effect is that as the campaign builds momentum, a major donor who has already made a pledge may be persuaded to increase the amount of the gift.

ENDOWMENT CAMPAIGNS

An endowment campaign is launched and run the same way as a capital campaign: a goal is set, donors are quietly contacted, and pledges are secured; once enough pledges are secured, the campaign is publicly announced.

Endowment campaigns are challenging, however, because the perceived benefit to the community is harder to demonstrate than that of a capital campaign. An endowment fund is a restricted fund that can provide either income for emergencies or a chunk of funds for a special project. Some organizations use a fixed percentage of their endowment for operating or annual programs as allowed by the terms of their endowment agreement. The board of directors generally votes on the restrictions applied to the endowment fund. Nonprofit experts will say that an organization's endowment should be at least twice its annual budget, and that it is best if it is five times as large. So if the Sunrise Charitable Foundation has an annual budget of $10 million, a comfortable endowment fund will be between $20 million and $50 million. While this is best practice, it surely doesn't always happen.

As I mentioned near the beginning of this book, the biggest university endowment is held by Harvard; as of this writing it is valued at $32 billion against an annual operating budget of roughly $4 billion. In other words, Harvard's endowment is eight times its operating budget.

To "sell" an endowment campaign takes a greater amount of persuasion than a capital campaign because there is no handsome new building or gleaming operating room to show donors as the goal. But with the right approach—and the right stories—donors can become enthusiastic about an endowment campaign. Furthermore, endowments are very often the beneficiaries of bequests; in their wills, donors often leave major assets to institutions in a restricted endowment fund.

GRANTS

Securing grants may be pursued as part of a campaign or on a project basis. Applying for and having a realistic chance of securing a grant from a funding agency (whether private, corporate, or governmental) is a painstaking process that should only be undertaken when there is a good chance of success. The first step is to determine whether the project is in perfect alignment with the granting history and guidelines of the agency. If it is, then the organization might go ahead and apply; in many cases, funding agencies will have highly detailed formats to which the application must conform. Some agencies have staff members who can help the nonprofit craft its application before the agency board votes on it. Many private foundations, however, provide little guidance, and you are forced to submit your application "blind." The foundation then informs you if you have been accepted or declined; that's all.

As a board member, you can be a huge help to the development staff by having a realistic view of grant making. Every development director can tell you—with exasperation—stories of some board member who, when grappling with the question of how to meet a budget goal, will demand, "Why don't we just get a grant?"

"We need new bathrooms—can't we just get a grant?"

"The exhibit is underfunded—let's just get a grant!"

"Our computers are old and out of date—aren't there grants out there for this?"

The answer is usually "No." Please trust your development staff— they are keenly aware of the grant-making universe. Grants are like matchmaking: the grantor (the foundation, corporation, or governmental agency making the grant) and the grantee (the nonprofit seeking the funds) have to be in perfect synch and, like finding your soul mate, it is hard to do. Not only do the grantee's requests have to fit the areas funded by the grantor to further its mission, but the timing has to be right as well.

Some foundations consider applications or request for proposals annually, semiannually, or quarterly; others may not have a prescribed timing and accept applications by invitation only. The notification periods for grants vary as well. A director of development may submit a grant application in June and not receive notification until September, December, or later.

In addition to all the stars that must be aligned for consideration, when an organization applies for a grant, it faces tremendous competition. As in individual fundraising, relationships matter, so if board members know grant makers, they should definitely talk to the development team. When it works, foundation support can be tremendous boon for an organization—providing necessary programmatic or operational support and even allowing a nonprofit to scale its size—but board members should be clear that grants are *not* easy fundraising solutions.

The Development Cycle

There is a life cycle to the process of acquiring major donations or grants. The graphic below illustrates this nicely.

For either soliciting a major gift from an individual or applying for a grant or corporate funding, the development cycle consists of six steps:

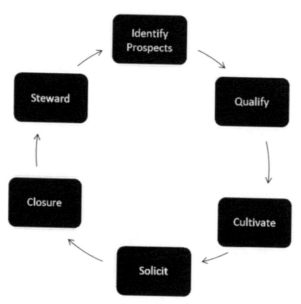

Major Gifts	Grants/Corporate Funding
Identify prospect	Identify funding agency
Qualify the prospect	Read guidelines carefully/Meet with grantor
Cultivate the prospect	Prepare application for grant
Solicit the gift	Submit application for grant
Close	Receive grant award
Steward the gift	Submit reports and communicate

Depending upon the prospect, the first five steps may be long or very brief. For example, with your friend Jennifer Adams, identifying and qualifying have already been done. Cultivation may consist of one meeting over coffee, or Jennifer may want to delve into the details of the project or take time to organize her finances.

The heart of successful fundraising is this process of donor prospecting and cultivation. For many small nonprofits, this is problematic because the development department is often insufficiently staffed to allow all the requisite development functions to be carried out.

While major events and annual campaigns may be both time and labor intensive, they are essential fundraising strategies for most nonprofits. The irony is that prospecting and cultivation are the areas that some organizations skimp on or ignore almost completely, however they are among the most important activities that nonprofits can do to ensure *sustainable* fundraising.

The development staff need not be solely responsible for prospecting and cultivation. The management team, the board, the development and related committee(s), and other stakeholders should play key and ongoing roles. What the development staff should do is put in place a formal mechanism for prospecting and tracking cultivation. Software is available to easily manage this process. Then either the staff or someone they delegate can manage the process and assignments. This is a relatively simple task but one that can yield real results and should not be overlooked.

As a board member, the key is to volunteer either to cultivate people already on the development director's radar or to think about people in your circles and those whom you meet and determine if they are prospects. Once you have determined that someone is a prospect— because he or she has affinity for the cause, financial resources, and a philanthropic mindset—you can communicate with the development director that you will take responsibility for cultivating the nonprofit's relationship with that prospect. It is very important that you report your progress to the staff person responsible for tracking relationships. When the time is right, you will move from cultivation to making a request. In the following chapter, we'll take a look at special events, which are often a very good first ask for prospects to bring them into the organization. ○

14

···

SPECIAL EVENTS

It's not just about being able to write a check. It's being able to touch somebody's life.

~ OPRAH WINFREY

Ah, the glitz and glamour of the nonprofit fundraising gala! Black ties and ball gowns on a starry summer evening, the orchestra playing, delicious food by a top caterer, perhaps a charity auction, and above all the promise of money being raised for the deserving hospital, museum, house of worship, or social-services provider. Today galas are often taken down a notch to weekday nights and business attire, but the purpose and key elements remain.

Fundraising events come in all shapes and sizes. These are some of the biggest:

- At over $415 million per year, Relay for Life from the American Cancer Society is the number-one fundraiser in the United States.

- The Susan G. Komen Race for the Cure raises a staggering $131 million to fight breast cancer.

- The Heart Walk raises nearly $100 million for the American Heart Association.

• The Met Gala, formally called the Costume Institute Gala, is the big annual fundraising gala for the benefit of the Metropolitan Museum of Art's Costume Institute in New York City. Widely regarded as one of the most exclusive social events in New York and one of the biggest fundraising nights of the city, it raised a reported $9 million in 2013 and a record of $12 million the following year.

Special fundraising events can be spectacular, but they can also be incredibly labor intensive and expensive. If your board is planning a big event, be aware of the costs involved, especially if the organization hires an outside event planner.

As a board member, you need to remember that the event's *net revenue* is more important than the *gross revenue*. Gross revenue is the total of all money brought in from a fundraising event (ticket sales, program ads, donations, revenues from an auction). But that figure is meaningless until you understand what it cost the organization to raise that money. These costs are both direct (catering, advertising, rentals, materials) and indirect (volunteer hours, overhead staff time). You don't know how much money you made until after you subtract the costs involved.

For example, Sunrise plans a gala with a band, catering, and an auction. For six months, one staff member spends half her time organizing the event, while a board committee provides oversight and helps sell tables. At the end of the event, the organization grosses $100,000, and it seems like a great success.

But that's the gross revenue. What was the net revenue of this gala? The direct expenses—the band, venue, catering, decorating, printing of invitations and the program, postage—cost $50,000. The *indirect* expenses include the resources of the organization that were committed to the event. The executive director made phone calls and attended meetings. The development director worked on the event. The staff member spent half a year preparing for this event, devoting half her daily working hours to it. Let's say the actual cost in terms of staff salaries was $20,000. That's $70,000 in actual cash costs for an event that grossed $100,000, making the net revenue $30,000.

This does not include in-kind contributions of time from the board committee, who put in many hours planning, promoting, and attending the event.

There will be costs associated with every fundraising event; the goal is to ensure that donors to the event understand that a significant portion of every dollar given will go to programs and services and not to event organizers, caterers, and decorators. Ideally, organizations can get event costs underwritten, and then all the money raised goes to support the cause.

What kind of event should you have? It could be nearly any activity for which people will pay money to participate. Ideally, your event should have some connection to the mission of the organization. For example, a well-known organization devoted to feeding the poor has an annual "Empty Bowl" event. Local artists donate hand-decorated bowls, and local restaurants donate simple one-pot foods. Patrons of the event buy an empty bowl and then fill it up with food.

Here are just a few of the most common types of fundraising events:

- Auction (live or silent)

- Bachelor/bachelorette auction

- Bingo

- Bowling

- Casino night (not real gambling, unless permitted by law)

- Celebrity roast

- Charity basketball

- Classic-car show

- Gala dinner dance

- Golf tournament

- Food sales (fish fry, barbecue dinners, etc.)

- Haunted house

- Concert or theatre show

- Raffle

- Walk/Run events

When discussing an event, be sure you ask these three questions:

1. What is the realistic amount that we will net from this event? Be sure to include all expenses and to be conservative in estimating sponsorships and attendees.

2. Do we have the bandwidth in terms of staff and volunteers to put on this event? If you do not have the internal staff to handle an event and will need to hire an outside event coordinator, planner, or additional staff of any kind, include this in the expenses.

3. What is the opportunity cost of this event? By doing this, what are you not going to be able to do because you will not have time nor staff? How many of your potential "asks" are you using for this event, and is this the best way to maximize their giving potential?

These three simple questions can save your organization a lot of time and disappointment. Don't be afraid to stop and ask!

ALCOHOL AT YOUR EVENT

If you are serving alcohol at your fundraising events, do not do it without careful forethought! Event hosts—including boards of directors—can be held responsible for the actions of their guests after they leave the event. You and/or the organization may be held responsible for injuries and damages that occur as the result of the alcohol you serve to a guest during your event. The conscientious host of a fundraising event where alcohol is served anticipates problems and puts safeguards in place.

Always verify that either the organization or your caterer or venue have the correct permits and licenses for the type of event you are hosting. It would be extremely embarrassing to have to cancel your expensive event because you failed to obtain the necessary permits. In many communities, the organization must obtain a special one-day liquor license. If in doubt, check in advance with your local police department. By "advance," I mean well before you send out the invitations! Do not wait until the last minute.

Make sure you take out the necessary insurance for your event and that the agent writing the policy knows that drinking will be involved. You may need to have a special insurance binder issued by their company naming you as an insured party.

If you are serving alcohol at your event, you may have to limit your guests to those who are of legal drinking age. During your event make sure all public entrances are manned by your staff and that they check the identification of anyone who looks underage. Another alternative is to issue plastic bracelets to attendees who are legally able to drink. Always use professional bartenders to serve the alcohol at your events. Professionals are insured and have TIPS training (Training for Intervention Procedures), which is education and training for the responsible service, sale, and consumption of alcohol. Many large fundraising events provide a free "sober ride" home for any intoxicated guest, using one of their local cab companies.

When the Party's Over...

Organizations have events for many different reasons. Most events can be categorized as primarily for fundraising, mission fulfillment, or outreach and engagement. It is important that once the event is over, you follow through, even though the next day all you want to do is return the rented chairs and tables before getting on with the rest of your life. Organizations too often say goodbye to the guests, clean up, write their thank-you notes, and check the event off the list.

If the event committee closes the book too soon, then you are not getting the most from your investment. Like many good parties, the action is at the *after-party*. The development director or staff member in charge of the event should conduct a proper after-party analysis, which should include these action steps:

1. Write thank-you notes to everyone. You certainly want to thank your honorees, speakers, special guests, donors, attendees, and committee. One often-overlooked group to thank is your vendors, especially if you enjoyed working with them and they did a good job. Handwrite as many notes as you can. As a nice touch, I like to send photos as keepsakes to honorees, speakers, special guests, and key donors.

2. Send out tax receipts. If you had an auction or such, you need to send people who purchased an item a receipt for tax purposes.

3. Submit post-event photos and video. Everyone loves pictures and videos. Send them to the daily, weekly, and monthly press. Put them on your website and social-media sites. Use them in your upcoming newsletters, both print and electronic.

4. Work the list of attendees and donors. What are the next steps for everyone who attended your event? Action plans for each person are the way to leverage your event and build on its success.

5. Celebrate and debrief with the staff and event committee. Have a meeting with your staff and committee to celebrate your success and talk about what worked, what didn't work, and what you would do differently if you held the event or a similar one again. Take written notes at this meeting and put them in your electronic and paper files. Your meeting should cover these topics:

- Review of logistics. Rate and review the venue, caterer, entertainment, transportation, audio-visual, and other expenses.

- Assessment of the event against its goals. For fundraisers, determine how much money was raised; for mission and outreach events, qualitative and quantitative assessment measures should be used.

- Discussion of the big picture. Review how the event fit into the organization's business and strategic plans. (This should be discussed before each event and then afterward to see if the concept and reality were on par.)

- Strategic follow-up. After sending thank-you notes and flowers, delve into the guest list and make note of guests and conversations of interest, those guests who expressed a desire to get more involved, and the organization's plan for following up.

- Give it a grade. Overall, what grade would you give the event? Would you repeat it? How would you change it? Why?

Planning a charity fundraising event can be a tremendous amount of work. There is a certain relief that planners feel when the event is over. Too often, though, other work is waiting in the wings that has been pushed aside or neglected. Resist the urge to move on before properly following up. Go the extra mile and evaluate your events thoroughly and be strategic in determining the next steps with attendees and donors.

Doing so will result in more thoughtful and higher-quality events and more friends, prospects, and donors. Having created and contributed to a successful fundraising event, as a board member you are ready to take responsibility for the long-range course of the organization, which is to get involved in strategic planning.

Special events are often highlights for a nonprofit. Next we will turn to more challenging times as we take a look at crises and challenges that nonprofits can face. ○

15

....

CRISES AND CHALLENGES: FINANCIAL, LEGAL, PR, AND MORE

The greatest threat to the not-for-profit sector is the betrayal of public trust, the disappointment of public confidence.

~ JOEL FLEISHMAN

As a member of the board of the Sunrise Charitable Foundation, you may experience nothing but smooth sailing over calm seas: no disasters, no scandals, and no conflicts. If that happens, be thankful and enjoy your tenure!

But we know that life is unpredictable, and there may come a time when the board must set aside routine matters and tackle a major challenge. By keeping a cool head, working cooperatively, and keeping your eye on the mission, you'll be able to work with your fellow board members, the staff, and other stakeholders to weather the storm and emerge stronger than ever.

Here's a review of some of the challenges that can confront the board. Some of them arise suddenly—a fire or illness—while others may be ethical issues that fester quietly before erupting. They all need to be dealt with quickly and decisively.

Financial Challenges

- Insufficient financial reserve or endowment to carry the organization through a lean period

- Emergency due to a calamity, such as a fire
- Bad economy or a recession (the Great Recession of 2008 inflicted great damage on many nonprofits when donations declined)
- Unexpected shortfall in a campaign or annual fund
- External factors resulting in dissipating funding, such as changes to current grant guidelines that prevent the organization from moving forward or the loss of a major donor due to death or relocation

Legal Problems

- Director giving the organization a loan, personally signing for a loan, or receiving a questionable loan
- CFO, controller, or executive director embezzling funds
- Self-dealing—the executive director or board committee hires a relative or awards a contract to company or related entity
- Cover-up of unethical or illegal actions

Public Relations Scandals

- Questionable personal conduct of a leader
- Actual harm done to a member or staff
- Financial impropriety, perceived or real
- Scandal involving the parent organization, even if the local chapter is not involved

External Issues

- Changing demographics eroding audience
- Competition from other attractions or providers
- Failure to plan in changing landscape or to anticipate change

Leadership Crises

- Lack of/Poor professional leadership
- Sudden death or illness of executive director or board chair

Toxic Environment

- Backbiting, accusations, or tension between the executive director and the staff and/or the executive director and the board

Sudden Opportunity

- Not all urgent matters are bad. For example, the building next door may suddenly come on the market, and the organization needs to move swiftly to acquire it.

The question of a toxic organizational culture is worth discussing because it is the kind of problem that can fester over time. Board members who become used to a toxic environment may think, "Well, that's just the way it is. There's nothing you can do about it." Not true! Not only can a toxic organizational culture be changed, it *must* be changed.

If your personal radar is working, you only have to spend a short period of time in an organization to get a feeling for the environment. Are the people who work there happy? Do they seem energetic or lethargic? Are they at ease or tense? Are people empowered to make decisions? Does the organization suffer from general malaise?

If the environment is unhealthy, there is often a toxic person contaminating the organization from above.

As noted by Peter Frost, author of *Toxic Emotions at Work: How Compassionate Managers Handle Pain and Conflict,* "The tone in an organization tends to be set from the top, and so toxicity is often a top-down phenomenon. As one human resources manager I interviewed observed: 'Fish stinks from the head!' The higher up the toxic person is, the more widely spread is the pain."

Toxic people in the workplace can wreak havoc. If toxic leaders are allowed to remain in place, they can cause an organization to be unproductive because of the culture of fear and tension they create and the energy that they exhaust. If healthy and highly competent people are not buffered from the toxicity, ultimately organizations run the risk of losing them. Over time, a toxic leader can incapacitate an entire organization.

Leaving a toxic leader in place is particularly dangerous for any organization with a high level of staff and client, volunteer, or donor interactions, as noxious fumes are difficult to contain.

Managers need to handle or seek help to contain those toxic individuals whom they supervise. When the dangerous behavior is coming from a CEO or executive director, the board must take action. This is yet another reason why it is important for the individual board members to have relationships with staff—so there can be channels for communication. Presidents and boards have to be willing to put on hazmat suits and deal with a toxic leader before that leader does permanent damage to the organization.

A toxic environment can be one where transgressions are actively committed, one where transgressions are swept under the rug, or a deadly combination of both. Here are three examples of how boards of directors can become caught up in toxic conflicts and crises—whether by their own making or because of the malfeasance of others.

THE MET COUNCIL

Sometimes a board is tipped off to a long-term problem that it may not have been able to spot without a whistleblower drawing the issue to their attention. When this happens, the board is duty bound to investigate. One hopes that the information is baseless, but if there is substance to the claim, swift action is necessary.

In September 2013, the *New York Post* reported the arrest of William Rapfogel, who had been the executive director of the well-respected Metropolitan Council on Jewish Poverty. According to the *Post*, " 'Breathtaking' is the word that the state comptroller, Thomas DiNapoli, used to describe the scheme of grand larceny that was formally laid against William Rapfogel," who had been fired from his job a month earlier.

Rapfogel was accused of signing inflated insurance contracts and then taking kickbacks from the insurance companies.

In court the following April, Rapfogel admitted stealing more than $1 million from Met Council, which he had led for more than two decades. Rapfogel confessed he had overseen a scheme for twenty years, colluding with the owner of an insurance company and two other executives at the charity to overcharge the Council for insurance policies and then skim off cash.

The scheme began to unravel in 2012 after the Met Council board received an anonymous letter detailing improprieties with insurance payments. Alerted to the possible crime, the Met Council board hired an outside law firm to investigate. The firm found evidence that the payments had been padded. Investigators said they found $400,000 in cash stashed in Rapfogel's homes.

In a statement, New York State Attorney General Eric T. Schneiderman said, "While New York has the greatest nonprofit sector in the country, this case reminds us that we must vigilantly protect it. ... I also thank the Met Council board of directors for bringing this activity to light and cooperating with our investigation."

Could this scandal have been detected sooner? Kickback schemes are not easy to spot, but perhaps more rigorous audits of the organization's expenses would have revealed the inflated prices the Council had been paying for insurance.

PENN STATE UNIVERSITY

When the Jerry Sandusky scandal erupted in 2011, Pennsylvania State University's board of directors hired former FBI director Louis Freeh, who became chairman of his own investigative firm, to look into how school officials handled the actions of assistant football coach Sandusky, who was later convicted of sexually assaulting ten boys.

Freeh's report, released in July 2012, found that "the most powerful leaders at the university," —university president Graham Spanier, senior

VP of finance and business Gary Schultz, the late head football coach Joe Paterno, and athletic director Tim Curley—"repeatedly concealed critical facts relating to Sandusky's child abuse from the authorities, the University's board of trustees, the Penn State community, and the public at large."

Even though the 267-page report was seen as providing victims with new ammunition to hold the university financially liable, the board embraced it. In response to the Freeh report, Karen Peetz, chair of Penn State's board of trustees, said the board "accepts full responsibility for the failures that occurred."

Evidence suggests that the board never knew of the accusations against Sandusky until the scandal exploded publicly. Without the assistance of a whistleblower (like the person who tipped off the Met Council), it is difficult to see how the board could have discovered the abuse cover-up. It was regrettable that the veneration of the Penn State football program led so many people to turn a blind eye and take the toxic attitude that the rights of the perpetrators carried more weight than the rights of the victims.

THE CHILDREN'S MUSEUM OF UTICA

In some unfortunate cases, the dysfunction and illegalities of an organization are so profound that headlines are generated, accusations made, and in the case of the Children's Museum of History, Science & Technology in Utica, New York, the state's attorney general launches an investigation.

The story hit the news in March 2014, when it was reported that the Children's Museum board of directors had unanimously voted to remove the chair, Christopher Gordon, from the board. Executive director Marlene Brown said it was because Gordon had been publicly discussing private museum business. Gordon said that he sought answers to what were called "other expenses" the museum had of roughly $50,000 a year between 2010 and 2012.

Nevertheless, it seems as though Gordon somehow remained in his position because a month later it was reported in the press that a group of members of the Children's Museum board of directors had suspended executive director Brown. In return, Brown said that she was not suspended and accused the leader of the group, the very same Christopher Gordon, of "committing fraud, out and out."

According to the *Utica Observer-Dispatch*, Gordon said that he was board chairman and that he was doing what a responsible board member should do. "We have the fiduciary responsibility as board members to know the finances of the museum," he explained. "We could be liable for anything in that building. Safety, finances."

A few weeks later, Oneida County District Attorney Scott McNamara confirmed that a formal investigation had been opened into financial transactions at the Utica Children's Museum.

In June, things only got worse for the museum. In a report, Utica Fire Chief Russell Brooks slammed the museum, calling the number and severity of fire and codes infractions "negligence." The final inspection report, obtained by the *Observer-Dispatch*, shows a twenty-page laundry list of violations. "I view this whole package as children being at risk, and also firefighters," Brooks said.

The institution's board split, with half supporting Marlene Brown and half calling for her ouster. Meanwhile, the museum closed its doors indefinitely for repairs.

Could this disaster have been avoided? Almost certainly. There's evidence that the board allowed some questionable financial arrangements to be created between the museum and the executive director and that the relationship between her and the board was simply too cozy for too long. And as for the fire-code violations, there's just no excuse for that—everyone was to blame, from the maintenance staff right up to the board chair. This board was not just wearing rose-colored glasses; it was wearing blinders.

Each of these examples involves crimes or poor behavior that could have been detected earlier if the board had been more aggressive in its oversight and if communications between the board and the top management of the organization had been more transparent and had reflected a culture of trust and respect.

A significant cause of board laxity is the understandable desire of its individual members to avoid conflict and strive for a smooth working partnership. Board members often view tension as a symptom of dysfunction, which everyone must try to avoid. Board service is viewed as something that should be pleasant and rewarding; the board member who "stirs the pot" by asking pointed questions may be seen as a malcontent. Staff frequently regards board members who have serious questions as obstacles or even enemies, and board members who are not big donors may be subtly discouraged from speaking up. As a result, some boards avoid their responsibilities and act as a rubber stamp for the executive director or board chair.

In your board service, if you sense any unethical or questionable practices at any level, speak up and demand transparency. Nonprofits are not privately held corporations; they are accountable to the government, to the community, to donors, and to the clients they serve.

And remember: A nonprofit is only as effective as its board! ○

16

SUCCESSION PLANNING AND
BOARD DEVELOPMENT

Before you are a leader, success is all about growing yourself.
When you become a leader, success is all about growing others.

~ JACK WELCH

No organization is static. Staff and board members retire, get promoted, or move away. New people come up through the ranks. A periodic changing of the guard—the succession of leaders and volunteers—is a necessary part of the life cycle of any organization. We see this in politics, in business, and in the nonprofit world.

At the Sunrise Charitable Foundation, after you have served on the board for a few years and weathered a few storms, you may be ready to take over as chair. Perhaps this is a position that you have been groomed to occupy, having served as vice-chair or in some other high-level post. Or, as is most likely the case with small nonprofits, the new board chair may simply be chosen from the pool of those current board members who are willing to take on the job.

THE LEADERSHIP DEVELOPMENT COMMITTEE

At the very beginning of this book I introduced you to the leadership development committee—the board committee charged with identifying and contacting potential board members and officers. The phone call from your friend on the leadership development committee conveyed the invitation to join the board of the Sunrise Charitable Foundation.

In seeking potential board members, the leadership development committee needs to take a strategic view and consider the big picture. Typically, the committee is responsible for a defined portfolio of activities that begins with developing and maintaining a list of eligible board candidates; people on the list may be current volunteers or prospects known to current board members. The committee contacts and interviews potential candidates, recommends candidates to the full board, and ensures each new board member receives induction and training.

In the course of its search, the committee will ask these questions:

- What skills and expertise are lacking on the board? Desirable skills needed on any board include budgeting, financial management, investments, human resources, legal matters, fundraising, special-events management, public relations, political connections, and marketing.

- Which of these skills can be taught through training, and which should the board seek in a new member?

- Does the composition of the board reflect the people served by the nonprofit? Is there gender and ethnic diversity on the board, and are a variety of viewpoints represented?

- Do our board members span the geographic reach of our membership, clients, and donor base?

- Are influencers and connectors in key social circles, the business community, and the philanthropic arena represented?

- Are there politicians, thought leaders, or local celebrities who add gravitas to the board and cause?

- Who will be the officers of the corporation and how does this slate fit with longer-term succession planning?

Succession Planning and Organizational Memory

Like large corporations, large nonprofits may have either tacit or formal succession plans. If there is a vice-chair, it may be understood that this person is next in line to be the chair. Sometimes the chain of logical succession can be disrupted by some overpowering reason, such as a board member making a donation that is historically enormous.

Ideally, the leadership development committee will have a pool of candidates who are at various levels of preparedness. Some may be ready to join the board, others may be qualified but temporarily unavailable, while others may be new to the organization and need more experience. As they rise through the ranks to positions of greater responsibility, leaders of nonprofit organizations need to have certain qualifications. They need leadership skills, financial skills, and a flair for diplomacy. Many of these skills are fungible—they can be used in any corporate environment. But they also must have two other attributes: passion for the unique mission of the organization and organizational memory.

Organizational memory simply means knowing how stuff gets done. People who have it know the details of the organization's everyday operations as well as the finer points of personal politics that can make an organization run smoothly. They know the history of the organization, and where it has been over the years. When something goes wrong, they know whom to call. They know people on the outside with whom the organization must deal with only occasionally, such as the local fire chief or city councilman.

People with organizational memory can occupy any position, from janitor to board chair. Since we are concerned with the nonprofit board, it goes without saying that the transfer of power from outgoing chair to incoming chair should be as smooth as possible; this implies that the incoming chair needs to be prepared in advance to take over and hit the ground running.

Here is the real secret to effective succession planning: It isn't just about knowing whom the next board chair or chairs will be. It's about having a strong board where everyone understands the big picture, is engaged, and knows his or her role. It's a board where there are clear procedures in place. The best succession plan is having a board that regularly operates under established professional practices; such a board will be able to continue to perform effectively regardless of whether the chairperson happens to be absent from one meeting or has unexpectedly announced that he or she is stepping down.

The Struggling Organization

If your organization struggles with succession, most likely the organization has other systemic challenges at hand. It may have solvency problems or perhaps a record of internal conflicts.

This becomes the classic chicken-and-egg problem. While you need a strong leader to tackle the organization's problems, the organization is not attractive to potential leaders because it is in trouble or at the very least is not healthy or robust. To compound the problem, the perception that you cannot get anyone to serve in a leadership role continually undermines the organization.

What is an organization to do?

Faced with this situation, many desperate organizations ask the current chair to stay on for an additional period of time or term. This short-term fix is advisable only if there's an ongoing project (such as a capital campaign or strategic restructuring) that will result in an ameliorated situation for the agency at the end of the term. In too many cases, organizations beg a checked-out president to hold over out of desperation. This is akin to treading water. It allows the organization to delay moving in a clear direction or with accelerated pace when that is exactly what is needed to make real progress.

In the alternative, boards and leadership development committees might consider putting together a council of invested leaders, past presidents, and/or long-term donors to act as a council of sages and to approach two people who have been involved with the organization (preferably but not necessarily current board members if allowed by the by-laws) to come in as co-chairs. They would do so with the understanding that the council was there to support and back them. People are more likely to take on a challenging role if they can share the responsibilities and have the advice and counsel of a wise, experienced group on which to rely.

REVITALIZING A STALE BOARD

Sometimes a board can become too set in its ways, too insular, or too comfortable; perhaps it lacks a deep bench of potential chairs. Such boards are prone to wearing rose-colored glasses or to allowing a dominant executive director or board chair to dictate the direction of the organization. Here are seven steps that can help any organization to assess its board and, if necessary, inject new talent.

1. Assess the current board and their attendance and engagement. Are there board members who should be removed before the term is over for egregious lack of involvement? Are there board members who should not be asked to serve again once their term is up?

2. Review the bylaws to determine the minimum and maximum number of board members required. How many open seats *must* the organization fill? How many more can it fill? If there are board members who should be removed before the term is over, are the criteria met for doing so and what is the process?

3. The executive committee and/or the leadership development committee should meet and consult with key stakeholders—staff, committee chairs, volunteers, donors, customers, and so on—to seek suggestions for potential board members. Simultaneously, a list of skill sets and other criteria sought in board members, such as geographical and network diversity, should be compiled. The names of prospective board members should be reviewed against the criteria list and ranked.

4. Hold an informational and social event about the organization and invite prospects to come and meet the current board and key stakeholders. Share the current vision for the organization and present opportunities for engagement. After the event, people with connections to particular prospects should follow up and gauge their interest.

5. Invite prospective board members to submit a brief indication-of-interest form that describes why they want to serve on the board; summarizes their past involvement with the organization (if any); describes their experience, strengths, areas of expertise, and perspective they will bring to the board; and indicates their willingness to comply with the specific delineated responsibilities and expectations of board members. Remember, it is very important for prospective board members to be told up front what the requirements of serving are (give or get, attendance at meetings, committee work) and what the expectations are beyond the requirements (attend programs and events, serve as ambassador of organization).

6. After reviewing the indication-of-interest forms, invite candidates you think would be a good fit for interviews with the leadership development committee. The goal of board composition is not to simply fill the seats. The goal for every board is to attract people who are passionate about the organization and its mission and who have time, energy, skills, and resources to serve.

7. Extend offers to join the board to those selected. It is also very important to make personal calls to all who submitted the indication-of-interest forms to thank them and look for other opportunities to engage them in the organization. Keep the door open for future board service.

If your organization is having problems attracting new, high-quality board members, it is the board's job to ask why and to address the underlying issues.

Board and Personal Development

In earlier chapters I touched upon board training and self-evaluation. While it may be possible to engage in self-evaluation and to create a program of board development, many boards engage the services of an outside consultant. My company's list of trainings is at the end of this book. The following are areas of training that might be provided by an outside consultant:

The Roles and Responsibilities of Board Members

In order for the organization to operate smoothly, it is important that all board members understand the governance structure and what board members are expected to do. Individuals new to the nonprofit arena should be familiarized with the ethics, compliance requirements, and nuances of working with volunteer organizations.

Management Skills

Board members may require training in key areas, such as strategic planning, overcoming conflicts, decision making, running meetings and evaluation. Other areas of study include identifying and rectifying problems and managing both organizational growth and financial contraction. Board members should be encouraged to share best practices from other successful nonprofit organizations.

Fundraising

Training in fundraising skills may include goal setting, storytelling, planning events, prospecting and cultivating relationships with donors, soliciting, and assessing the effectiveness of fundraising programs.

Aside from formal training that you might receive, serving on a nonprofit board can provide you with an environment that stimulates personal development. For example, one responsibility of being on a board is raising awareness and funds for the organization. By doing so, you'll have the opportunity to connect with supporters from a variety of places. By connecting with all of these people, you can get their assistance in pushing your organization forward. If you are forward thinking, you will cultivate these connections and bring them into your personal network.

By serving on a board, you will expand your network and acquire new competencies, knowledge, and experiences that will apply to your full-time work. Your committee work may mean you will learn how to manage projects and teams in order to help move the organization forward. These skills will transfer over into your professional life as you find yourself being as clear as possible about strategy and goals while also striving to be kept accountable as you keep your co-workers accountable. Gaining leadership experience and growing your leadership style through nonprofit positions can be good for your career both in terms of what you learn and the visibility you receive. Be sure to add your board service to your resume and LinkedIn profile.

Besides working on a cause you are passionate about and the fulfillment and camaraderie that comes through service, there are tangible professional benefits to serving on a board ○.

17

GETTING OFF THE BOARD

*I don't know what your destiny will be, but one thing I do know:
The only ones among you who will be really happy are those who
have sought and found how to serve.*

~ ALBERT SCHWEITZER

It is possible that your service on the board of the Sunrise Charitable Foundation will be so personally rewarding to you (and that there will be an absence of mandated term limits) that you end up serving on the Sunrise board until the very day that you are ushered into your new residence in the retirement home.

It's possible, but not very likely. Regardless of how pleasurable your service is, there will almost certainly come the day when you are going to leave the boardroom at Sunrise for the last time. Farewells will be said, and there might even be a little party with heartwarming speeches, but it will be time to go.

This will happen most likely as the result of one of three circumstances.

1. You've Reached Your Maximum Term Limit

If you need to rotate off the board because you have no choice, then graciously accept the board's fond farewells and be on your way. Some boards may allow you to re-join after a year or two off; if so, that's a choice that you can make. You may also choose to stay involved with the organization as a volunteer (some organizations have an advisory board or leadership council); your expertise and your contributions will no doubt be welcomed.

2. It's the End of Your Term, and You're Not Seeking Another Term

If you've been happy in your service, you don't owe anyone a detailed personal explanation. You can just say, "It's been a pleasure and a delight to serve, and I look forward to the next chapter in my life." If you want to offer a reason, fine. Your reason could be one of the following:

"My regular job has become too demanding."

"We plan to move this summer."

"I'm getting involved in too many other activities."

"The kids need me at home."

"The hour-long drive to get here is just too much."

"My mother is ill, and I need to cut back."

The question becomes stickier if you are not continuing forward because you are unhappy with some aspect of the organization or the board. If that's the case, it is your decision whether or not you want to make this known. You may choose to simply walk away and not leave a parting message. Or you may sincerely believe that by saying something you can affect positive change. Only you can decide this.

But if you are at odds with the board and you are not comfortable staying, leave gracefully but with dignity. Consider writing a letter to the board explaining your position and asking to have it entered into the minutes. The board members who were absent at the meeting will have access to your message, and in the future the record of the issue you address may help the board.

If you simply feel ineffective as a board member, think about why that is so and articulate your viewpoint in your letter.

If you are not continuing because of a reason that involves your relationship with the organization, first privately inform the board chair, then the executive director, and then the entire board. If you will be attending one more meeting, be sure to express your good will. Your fellow board members will be listening carefully to your departing words, so don't burn your bridges; take advantage of the moment to make a positive contribution to the organization and its cause.

3. You Leave Before Your Term Is Over

This can happen because of a change in your life (you have a new job, you're moving away, you have a new baby, your mother is ill). It may happen because you miscalculated the commitment required; perhaps you've missed several board or committee meetings and you feel it is unfair to remain. It may happen because, sadly, you have a conflict or problem with the organization or the board.

If you have concerns about the organization or the executive director but haven't yet voiced them, consider raising them to the board chair before finalizing your decision to resign. You can privately say, "The real reason I am resigning is because I'm just not on the same page as Susan, the executive director. While I can't work constructively with her, I don't want to prevent the rest of the board from moving ahead with her."

If you have a problem with the board chair, you may want to privately express yourself to a trusted board member. Once again, these are decisions that only you can make based upon your individual circumstances.

Through serving on the board, it is likely that you will make connections with the staff, other board members, donors, and constituents. Hopefully, these relationships will continue after your term ends and so will your commitment to the mission and organization overall, whether as a donor, a volunteer, or a friend.

NEXT STEPS

Nonprofit board service is a wonderful way to perform meaningful work, expand your personal and professional networks, acquire new skills, and be part of a purposeful enterprise. It is exciting to be part of a strong board or one on an upswing. And once you know what a good board looks like, boards that are dysfunctional become easy to spot.

Like many other scenarios, you get what you put into it. The more deeply you dive in and the more you become engaged and involved, the more of an impact you can have.

In this book we have discussed how to evaluate the invitation to join a board, outlined the responsibilities of the board and how the board works, described the funding and workings of a nonprofit, previewed strategic planning, sketched who is on the team, highlighted pitfalls to avoid, and explored possible paths for your development and leadership as a board member.

What's next for you? How are you going to use your newfound knowledge? What are your action steps?

Let's continue the conversation. I want to hear from you and help if I can. I'd love to know what you decide, and why; whether board service is a good fit for you; what your challenges have been; and what parts you've found most rewarding.

To quote Michael Bloomberg, "I've always respected those who tried to change the world for the better, rather than just complain about it."

Nanette Fridman
Founder and Principal, Fridman Strategies
E-mail: fridmanstrategies@gmail.com
Twitter: @NanetteFridman
Facebook: https://www.facebook.com/FridmanStrategies
LinkedIn: www.linkedin.com/in/nanettefridman/
Website: www.fridmanstrategies.com

Fridman Strategies Training Offerings

I hope that you found *On Board: What Current and Aspiring Board Members Must Know About Nonprofits and Board Service* to be informative and useful. If your organization would benefit from customized trainings on any of the topics covered in the book, please contact me by visiting my website at www.fridmanstrategies.com or directly by e-mail at fridmanstrateges@gmail.com.

Below is a sampling of successful training topics that I have delivered during retreats or as part of series or individual training sessions to professionals and volunteers of nonprofits. Many organizations select a series of trainings for their boards or subsets over a period of time. All trainings are designed to meet specific goals and are customized for each organization. Trainings can be in person or virtual to meet every budget.

Board Development
- Nonprofit Governance Models that Work
- Roles and Responsibilities of Board Members of Nonprofit Organizations
- Secrets of Highly Effective Boards
- Empowering Working Committees
- Building the Board of the Future: Leadership Development, Nominating and Succession Planning Today
- Secret Strategies of Board Chairs and Executive Directors with Powerful Partnerships

Fundraising
- Effective Ways that Board Member Can Help Raise Funds without Ever Asking for Money
- Formulating a Successful Financial Resource Development Plan

- Fundamentals of Development: The Basics Every Board Should Understand
- Solicitation Training
- Running a Major Gifts Campaign
- Storytelling for Fundraising
- Best Practices for Obtaining Grants from Private and Corporate Foundations
- Win-Win Corporate Partnerships
- Tips and Tricks for Extraordinary Events
- The Relationship between Evaluation and Fundraising

Organizational and Staff Development

- Key Performance Indicators for Nonprofit
- Paradise by the Dashboard Light: How Nonprofits Can Use Dashboards to Monitor Organizational Wellness
- Measuring Success: Monitoring Progress and Evaluation
- Fostering Organizational Cultures for Success
- The Role of Mentoring at Work
- Learning to Coach for Managers
- The Importance and Process of Meaningful Employee Evaluations
- Middle Managers: The Challenges of Managing Up and Down
- It's about Time: Time Management to Achieve Your Goals
- Mapping Your Organization's Micro-Communities
- Bringing Innovation into Mature Organizations

Strategic Planning

- What Is Strategic Planning? and Why Does My Organization Need to Do It?
- Designing the Right Strategic Planning Process
- Increasing the Impact of Your Strategic Planning Efforts
- How to Keep Your Strategic Plan off the Shelf

Strategic Restructuring

- Building Effective Collaborations and Strategic Alliances
- Organizational Dating or Marriage? Making Sense of the Best Options from Collaboration to Merger for Your Organization
- Overview and Considerations for Nonprofit Mergers or Consolidations
- Cultivating and Evaluating Prospective Partners ○

Acknowledgements

My sincere thanks to the many nonprofit board members and professional staff whom I have had the privilege to work with and learn from over the last twenty-five years. Your dedication and hard work is inspirational and motivational.

Many people have provided me with helpful insights about the third sector: Joslyn Arnon, Emily Ausbrook, Simi Kaplin Baer, Emely Martinez Cockrell, Aaron Dworkin, Laura Fish, Marla Gay, Rachel Glazer, Elyse Hyman, Diane Knopf, Lisa Nagel, Julie Newburg, Ben Paul, Duffy Page, Ila Sidman Sabino, Maria Samiljan, Betsy Cohen Sandler, Guy Sapirstein, Barbara Schneider, Debbie Sussman, Jennifer Weinstock, Dee Dee Witman and Nina Wright.

I am extremely grateful to my early readers for their comments: Peter Edelman, Laura Fish, Elyse Hyman, and my longest serving editor-in-chief, Beverly Loebenberg.

Thank you to Thomas Hauck for his early help getting started and to Lisa Thompson for designing the cover and laying out the book. I appreciate Neil Peller and Barbara Peller's help polishing and proofreading.

Working with my client on her book taught me so much. Thanks Helene Naftali for the tutorial.

My sincere gratitude to Lisa Abbate of WordMountain.com for her insights, editorial expertise, and indispensable guidance throughout the tremendous process of publishing this book.

My professional women's group is a wonderful source of laughter, connections and encouragement. I am glad that Sheryl Sandberg brought us together.

It takes a village to be a working parent, and I am grateful for my villages both on the north shore and in Newton.

And finally, special thanks to my biggest supporters in this endeavor and life. I am very lucky to have such amazing friends and family. To my wonderful husband Jose, thank you for encouraging me to do the work that I am passionate about and for being my partner on the incredible journey of life. To my children, Jacob and Alexis, I am so proud of the incredible people you are. Never stop learning or caring about your communities and the world around you, and remember to do your part to make them better. To my mother, Beverly Loebenberg, thank you for making sure that I had an excellent education and strong foundation and for teaching me the importance of list making. To my father, Ted Loebenberg, thank you for the genetic chutzpah that has allowed me to be myself and forge my own path. ○

ABOUT THE AUTHOR

Nanette R. Fridman has a long history in the nonprofit sector. She founded Fridman Strategies to assist nonprofit organizations with the strategies, structures, and training to advance their missions and maximize their impact. Nanette Fridman's practice primarily focuses on strategic planning, governance, financial resource development, and leadership coaching. Her clients range from small start-ups to large international organizations. Nanette is also a sought-after, dynamic public speaker, known for informing, energizing, and motivating audiences.

Before founding Fridman Strategies, Nanette was a corporate attorney at Mintz Levin Cohn Ferris Glovsky and Popeo, PC. Prior to her legal career, Nanette was the national field director for an advocacy organization in Washington, D.C.

Originally from Rhode Island, Nanette earned her Juris Doctorate, cum laude, and Masters in Public Policy from Georgetown University. She received her BA, summa cum laude, in political science from Tufts University and was elected to Phi Beta Kappa. Nanette also studied at the Hebrew University in Jerusalem. Nanette is honored to be a Harry S. Truman Scholar and has received numerous other academic, professional, and philanthropic awards for her work.

A serial social entrepreneur and perpetual grassroots organizer, Nanette has served on many nonprofit boards and trained thousands of individuals. She lives in Newton, Massachusetts, with her husband Jose and their children, Jacob and Alexis. ⟡

For more information, visit:
www.fridmanstrategies.com

BIBLIOGRAPHY

American Institute of Philanthropy. "Top 25 Compensation Packages." Last Updated January 16, 2014. Accessed April 14, 2014.
<http://www.charitywatch.org/hottopics/Top25.html >.

Averkamp, Harold. "Balance Sheet." Accessed June 13, 2013.
<http://www.accountingcoach.com/balance-sheet/explanation>.

Barnes Foundation, The. Accessed September 25, 2014.
<http://www.barnesfoundation.org/about/>.

"Barnes Foundation." Accessed October 3, 2014.
<http://en.wikipedia.org/wiki/Barnes_Foundation>.

Blackwood, Amy S., Katie Roeger, and Sarah Pettijohn. "The Nonprofit Sector in Brief: Public Charities, Giving, and Volunteering, 2013." Accessed November, 24, 2012.
<http://www.urban.org/UploadedPDF/412674-The-Nonprofit-Sector-in-Brief.pdf>.

Board Café. "The Right Way to Resign from the Board." CompassPoint Nonprofit Services. Accessed October 15, 2007.
<http://www.compasspoint.org/board-cafe/right-way-resign-board>.

Bohse & Associates, Inc. "Non-Profit Board Statistics." *Bohse Tips: Board of Directors Series* (2007). Accessed August 22, 2014.
<http://bohse.com/images/file/Board_of_Director_Series/Non-Profit_Board_Statistics.pdf>.

Boris, Elizabeth T., Erwin De Leon, Katie Roeger, and Milena Nikolova. "2010 National Survey of Nonprofit-Government Contracting and Grants." Accessed September 25, 2014.
<www.urban.org/publications/412227.html>.

Brengle, Deane. "Are You Serving Alcohol at Your Fundraising Event?" Accessed February 22, 2014.
<http://www.fundraising-newsletters.com/are-you-serving-alcohol-at-your-fundraising-event.html>.

Carey, Jack. "Penn State Board Takes 'Full Responsibility' for Failures." *USA Today*. Accessed July 12, 2012.
<http://content.usatoday.com/communities/campusrivalry/post/2012/07/penn-state-board-takes-full-responsibility-for-failures/1#.VCRMS0vob9A>.

Catchafire. "About Catchafire." Accessed October 3, 2014.
<https://www.catchafire.org/about/>.

Cooper, Elizabeth. "Fire Chief: Children's Museum Violations 'negligence.'" Last Updated June 2014. Accessed April 3, 2014.
<http://www.uticaod.com/article/20140601/News/140539871>.

Corporation for National and Community Service. "Volunteering and Civic Engagement in the United States." Accessed September 25, 2014. <http://www.volunteeringinamerica.gov/national>.

Davidson, Paul S. and Tera Rica Murdock. "Legal Duties and Avoiding Liability: A Nonprofit Board Member Primer." *Trustee Magazine.* Accessed October 3, 2013. <http://www.trusteemag.com/display/TRU-news-article.dhtml?dcrPath=/templatedata/HF_Common/NewsArticle/data/TRU/WebExclusives/2013/webexclusive0613legalduties>.

"District Attorney Investigating Children's Museum." *Utica Observer Dispatch.* Last Updated April 18, 2014. <http://www.uticaod.com/article/20140418/News/140419273>.

Donovan, Doug, Ben Gose, and Maria Di Mento. "Gifts Surge From the Wealthiest U. S. Donors." *The Chronicle of Philanthropy.* Accessed February 9, 2014. <http://philanthropy.com/article/Gifts-Surge-From-Rich-U-S/144601/>.

Frost, Peter. *Toxic Emotions at Work: How Compassionate Managers Handle Pain and Conflict.* Cambridge: Harvard Business School, 2003.

Ganz, Marshall. "Why Stories Matter," *Sojourners Magazine,* Mar. 2009. Web. Accessed September 25, 2014. <http://sojo.net/magazine/2009/03/why-stories-matter>.

Grant Thornton's Not-for-Profit and Higher Education Practices. "2012 National Board Governance Survey for Not-for-Profit Organizations." Accessed September 25, 2014. <http://www.grantthornton.com/staticfiles/GTCom/Not-for-profit%20organizations/Board%20Governance%20SurveyNational_Board_Governance_Survey_NFP_Organizations_2012_Final.pdf>.

Harvard Kennedy School. "Women and Public Policy Program." Accessed October 6, 2014. <http://projects.iq.harvard.edu/wappp/how-join>.

Hendershot, Neil L. "'No Standing for Barnes Foundation Petitioners." PA Elder, Estate & Fiduciary Law Blog. Last Updated May 19, 2008. <http://paelderestatefiduciary.blogspot.com/2008/05/no-standing-for-barnes-foundation.html>.

Heutel, Garth and Richard Zeckhauser. "The Investment Returns of NonProfit Orgnanizations, Part 1, Tales from 990 Forms." Last Updated February 21, 2013. http://www.hks.harvard.edu/fs/rzeckhau/EndowmentsPaperPartI.pdf>.

Horton, J. Lloyd. "Emerging Issue: When Is a Pledge Legally Binding?" Association of Fundraising Professionals. Accessed October 3, 2014. <http://www.afpnet.org/Ethics/EmergingIssuesDetail.cfm?itemnumber=4220>.

"Knowledge Base." Foundation Center. Accessed February 6, 2014. <http://www.grantspace.org/tools/Knowledge-Base/Nonprofit-Management/Boards/legal-duties-of-the-nonprofit-board>.

La Piana, David. "Boards Should Only Have Three Committees." Blue Avocado. Last Updated June 7, 2009. <http://blueavocado.org/content/boards-should-only-have-three-committees>.

Lipsky, Seth. "The Met Council Scandal & NY's Nonprofit Nightmare." *New York Post.* Accessed September 25, 2013. <http://nypost.com/2013/09/25/the-met-council-scandal-nys-nonprofit-nightmare/>.

Mayo Foundation for Medical Education and Research. "Mayo Clinic Mission and Values." Mayo Clinic. Accessed September 24, 2014. <http://www.mayoclinic.org/about-mayo-clinic/mission-values>.

Moran, William J. "Hiring a New Nonprofit Executive Director." The Moran Company. Accessed July 12, 2014. <http://www.morancompany.com/hiring-a-new-executive-director>.

Pogrebin, Robin. "Met Opera Receives a Record $30 Million Gift." 26 Mar. 2010. *The New York Times.* Accessed June 16, 2014. <http://www.nytimes.com/2010/03/27/arts/music/27gift.html>.

Robert, Henry M. *Robert's Rules of Order.* New York: William Morrow and Company, 1971.

Roberts, Daniel. "Louis Freeh on Penn State." *Fortune.* Last Updated July 25, 2013. <http://fortune.com/2013/07/25/louis-freeh-on-penn-state/>.

Roeger, Katie L., Amy Blackwood, and Sarah L. Pettijohn. *The Nonprofit Almanac.* Washington, D.C.: Urban Institute, 2012.

"Sector's Economic Impact | Independent Sector, The." Independent Sector. Last Updated June 9, 2010. <www.dsf.state.ct.us/cfpc/lib/cfpc/volunteer_time_s%3Dvolunteer_t.pdf>.

Sturgis, Alice. *The Standard Code of Parliamentary Procedure.* New York: McGraw-Hill, 2001.

Strauss, Gary. "Company Directors See Pay Skyrocket." *USA Today.* Last Updated October 26, 2011. <http://usatoday30.usatoday.com/money/companies/management/story/2011-10-25/director-compensation-rising/50918332/1>.